CONTENTS.

CHAPTER I.

Conversation with his physician, and his indifference about death—The minister sent for—Prayer—Meditation on life—Age of Reason—A swoon—Sees a spirit—The effort of the spirit to identify herself—His death—Funeral services—Doubting minister—Conversation with his spirit companion—Benediction, and opinions of the people—The end of wonders—Joy in his new sphere—The greeting—The woman and the doctor—His mother—Her welcome—His grave—The thoughts of the grave digger—Anxiety to reveal the truth—Promise to him of a coming time when it could be done with safety to mediums—Origin of sight—Thoughts of minds at his grave—Disclaims intentional wrong—Objections to religion—Visit to the minister—Conversation between the minister and servant—Prayer—Servant complains—Cheering conversation of Paine and his companion—Proposes to relate his experience, and signs his name.—[From page 13 to page 27.]

CHAPTER II.

Pleased with his new life—Recognition of rudimental associates—Reason why Paine's writings were unpopular—His opposition to revelation considered—Penn makes an effort to show Paine his error, but was defeated—Error acknowledged—Strife about opinions condemned—Nature is never contradictory, but just—All wrong induced by ignorance—Remedy for wrongs—Wisdom peaceful—The will of resistance—The principles of nature enforced—Education in wrong the cause of wrong—Non-resistance advocated—Penn takes him to a temple—Enters an arch-door—Initiation into wisdom—Assumes an obligation—A new song is sung—Receives a lesson—Description of the temple—Name recorded—A book opened—Banner unfurled—Words on the banner—Explanation of justice, wisdom, progression, order and harmony—Duties enjoined—Charge of the master—Emblems explained—Master and servant — Freedom of servants — Obedience to nature demanded — Implements of masonry — Proof of masonry — The High Priest instructs — The book opened and read — Interpretations forbidden — Repentant mind — Conducted to the inner court — The white stone — Name changed — Receives a new baptism — An anthem and ode were sung — The temple by whom made, and its pillars — Hears a wail of sorrow, and prepares for a mission.— [From page 27 to page 52.]

CHAPTER III.

The Cottage — Landlord impressed — Efforts of spirits — Maniac threatens his family — Landlord advises to send for the minister — Wife wants a doctor — Iron moved by a spirit — Nobleman and Mary confounded by the sounds—Attributes the sounds to satan and witches—Becomes agitated—Boasts of English courage—Gives Mary a half crown — Sends for a physician—Maniac grows more ill—Tea and sugar bought—The doctor comes and prescribes—Aid promised—Curate required to pray at his home—The maniao dies—Grief of Mary—Parental counsel at the time of her marriage repeated—Her husband buried—The family taken to the Alms-house—Affecting conversation between the mother and her son—The overseer questions Mary—Oppression of the poor—Voluntary and involuntary servitude explained.— [From page 52 to page 64.]

CHAPTER IV.

The Castle described—The centurion alarmed—Faith proved by works—Interpretations of the Bible disallowed—Penn called an infidel—Dialogue between the centurion and Penn—Teacher called—Dialogue continued —Theological opinions the cause of strife and wrong—Paine and Penn retire—Conversation between them—Witnesses beheaded—Dialogue between the Teacher and his Master—A wheel within a wheel—Gold and silver the motive power—Attraction of affinities—Fear and hope make slaves—The king's palace—Conversation between Thomas and William —Grand Master instructs Thomas—A new song—Consistency wrong when minds are wrong—Experience the proper test of principles—Some minds serve two masters—Works justify—Repentance is salvation—Departure for the Temple.— [From page 64 to page 102.]

LIGHT FROM THE SPIRIT WORLD.

THE

PILGRIMAGE

OF

THOMAS PAINE,

AND OTHERS,

TO THE SEVENTH CIRCLE

IN

THE SPIRIT WORLD.

REV. C. HAMMOND, Medium.

CHAPTER V.

Unity of work — Each receives a penny — Visits another temple — The Master's charge to Thomas — Advice of the chief — Counsel of the commander — Explanation of the helmet, spear, sword with two edges, arrows and bow, sling and pebbles — Trumpet — Directions to revisit the castle.— From page 102 to page 110.]

CHAPTER VI.

The deacon's prayer — Thomas and Mary converse — Dialogue between the deacon and Thomas on rewards, a day of judgment, and the atonement — The deacon converted — Sung the new song — Departure for the temple — The deacon initiated into the mysteries of wisdom, and the secret explained — Thomas and the deacon revisit the castle.— [From page 110 to page 126.]

CHAPTER VII.

The wonder in the castle—Dialogue between the chief, the deacon, and Thomas — The senior consulted — The circle of the temple summoned by the trumpet — Conversation between the Commander of the temple and the senior of the castle on war — On rights — The conversion of 24 elders, and 144,000 — The Commander conducts them to the temple, where they were initiated into that degree of wisdom.— [From page 126 to page 144.]

CHAPTER VIII.

Mission of Thomas and the elders — The king and guard — The elder addresses the king — Conversation with him — He refuses wisdom — A dialogue with a mind on fear — Calls a great multitude to hear the elder — Address of the elder — Conversation with the circle — Imputed righteousness — A thousand times ten thousand converted, and received into the temple.— [From page 144 to page 165.]

CHAPTER IX.

Thomas finds two minds wrangling — Enters into conversation with them — Refuses to give his name — Opposes teaching what the teacher does not know — Opposes controversy — Rejects innate depravity — Discards wrong views —Recommends facts for opinions — Explanation of sun and moon, which stood still by the command of Joshua — Nature instructs mind — Wrangling unwise — Wisdom will overcome wrong — Freedom induces righteousness — Masters responsible for the doings of servants —Another mind is converted — The work of the temple harmonious — Duty to avoid discord — The assent is gained — The convert sees a light — William gives him advice, and conducts him to the temple, when he receives a new name, and a white stone.— [From page 165 to page 186.]

CHAPTER X.

Receives a visit from a superior mind — Proposition to advance accepted — The seraphim sings — A pearl given — Enters a world of light and song — Description of the works which he saw — The instruction of the Worthy — The song of the free — Address of another mind on the key of wisdom — The seven seals — Address of a third mind — Conducts to the sixth circle — A lecture on social progress — Hope a reality — A lecture on prophecy — Rules of prophecy the same as mathematical — Prediction of communicating with the inhabitants of earth — Predictions, opinions only of those below the sixth circle—A lecture on purity and prophecy—Nature the standard by which to determine right and wrong —Advancement to the seventh circle, or court of Beauty—Sees a white throne and inscriptions—A little child leading a lion—A serpent fastened to a rock—Twenty four pillars of wisdom—Minstrels chant a welcome—Emblems explained Prediction of events now taking place—Contemplated mission to the rudimental sphere, and how it would be received—The serpent to be destroyed—Evils to be overcome by wisdom.— From page 186 to page 235.]

CHAPTER XI.

Franklin, Swedenborg. Paine. and his companions visit a place near the castle — Old things become new — Process of change — Identity preserved — Self is a part of the body — All sympathize together in good and ill — Governments defective — Opposition to capital punishment — Origin of evil — How overcome — Success of the mission — Means must be adapted to conditions — Contradictory communications develop the condition of minds in the second sphere — Conflicting revealments harmonious with different degrees of wisdom —Writing mediums—Societies and forms of worship —Adaptation is harmony —Harmony should not be disturbed —The mission of spirits will be to regulate minds —Minds will change forms —Retire to a mansion —Onward is a passport —Dullness reproved —Dedication of the Pilgrimage.— [From p. 235 to p. 259.]

PREFACE.

AGREEABLY to announcement in the "Light from the Spirit World," I am able to present this volume to the public, under circumstances which will be gratifying to all those who are the friends of Progress and Reform. No pains have been spared to present the precise words chosen by the author, and preserve the style and sense of the original manuscript. In regard to the merits of the production, it must speak for itself; for, whatever of merit or demerit it may possess, I am worthy of neither praise nor censure. Astounding as may be the assertion, that I had no will to write it, or exercised any other control, than to let my hand be moved by an invisible influence, and write as it would, without any volition on my part, yet it is, nevertheless, true. And, I am quite confident, that out of the two thousand writing mediums, now in the United States, no one in a passive condition will be able to contradict the assertion. Indeed, I have found by actual experiment, that, in a great many instances, the spirit who controls my hand, has succeeded in writing sentences contrary to my will, and while I was endeavoring with all my volition, to write something else.

But, so far as the orthography and punctuation of the Pilgrimage are concerned, I have exercised supervision. And yet, much aid has been afforded me by spirits in this matter. They arranged all the paragraphs and sentences. The initials, which represent different minds, were added by myself, to aid the general reader; and also the division of the work into chapters, with the prefatory contents of the same. Never having written a book in my life, excepting with the control of spirits, who have now given two volumes to the public, in about eight months, it may occur to the reader, that other divisions would have been preferable; but I have made the divisions as they seemed to me most natural.

This work has been written with uncommon despatch. Consequent upon the issue of the "Light," in November, 1851, I was seemingly wearied with letters on business and inquiries, in regard to matters connected with spirit developments; so that, in the brief period of four months, I have received about two hundred, which demanded reading and reply. This necessarily absorbed much of my time; especially, as very many solicited information from spirits.

Near the close of December, 1851, I began to sit for this work. I found my engagements such that I could only devote a part of each day, and this part was frequently interrupted by strangers who desired information on the subject. But the interruption did not seem to disconcert the writer. Though often breaking off in the middle of a sentence, the spirit knew exactly where to commence, even without any reading of what had been written. Notwithstanding these embarrassments, I found on the first of February, 1852, that my manuscript was nearly equal to the desired contents for a book; at which time, I entered into an arrargement with the publisher, Mr. Dewey, by which I am able to give this work a more extended circulation, and at less cost, than I otherwise could have done, which I trust will be abundantly obvious in its mechanical execution and neatness.

Concerning my condition while writing this book, I will say, that when writing, the whole subject matter was entirely in the dark to me. I would take my pen, and place myself in the attitude of writing, when all thought and care would be wholly abstracted from my mind. As my thoughts vanished, my hand would generally begin to move, and a word would be written. Then I would know what that word was. When the first word was written, my hand would be uplifted so as to leave a space between the words, and proceed as before. In this way the book was written. But when the spirit chose, I found my mind often, very often, though not always, impressed with the word which was being written. And some mediums inform me that whole sentences are impressed upon their minds at once; but with me it is a rare thing that I have more than one word at a time, and that comes, as it were, while they are writing it.

Should the reader receive the instruction and pleasure from a perusal of these pages, which I have while they were being written, the reward will be very great. I shall condemn no one if they do not read it, because, in my opinion, they will suffer sufficient loss without it. There are none who need the consolation and reform which spirits require, more than those who refuse to be instructed by them; but there are many who will, as they have done, aim their darts at both. They belong to a circle who deserve pity more than censure.

With the history and death of Thomas Paine, I know nothing, save what has been written by an invisible influence with my hand. Having been connected with the ministry for over twenty two years, I was not inclined to read his productions; and since I have become a writing Medium, I have found no leisure to read any book. In fact, my taste for reading the productions of human wisdom is all absorbed in the divine. The spirit proposes to write another volume, and when it is written, it will be published.

The Diagram will serve to explain the circles of wisdom, as enjoyed by minds in heaven. There are minds in the body who occupy the first, second, third, and fourth circle, according to this diagram. But I would inform the reader, that whatever may be the circle to which minds belong, in the rudimental or second sphere, it does not separate one from another by an impassable partition, so that one can not hold intercourse with another, though occupying different circles. As different circles in the body may converse together, so different circles in the spirit world may do the same. The circles do not represent arbitrary lines of division between spirits, but simply degrees of wisdom. That the higher circles mingle with the lower, for the purpose of making them wiser, is apparent from the whole body of this work. I consider, therefore, that circles express the degrees of wisdom and bliss which each spirit is qualified, as it is developed, to enjoy, and not as forming a line of separation among the inhabitants of heaven. The wisdom of heaven differs essentially from the wisdom of earth, in regard to the real merits of the mind, and its qualifications for enjoyment.

The style of some parts of this volume is unusual. A circle is sometimes addressed in the singular number, where it would seem to require the plural; but this departure from grammatical accuracy, may be justified on the ground, that the circle were all of one mind, or sentiment.

C. HAMMOND.

ROCHESTER, March, 1852.

DIAGRAM,

REPRESENTING THE DIFFERENT CIRCLES AND SPHERES

IN THE SPIRIT WORLD.

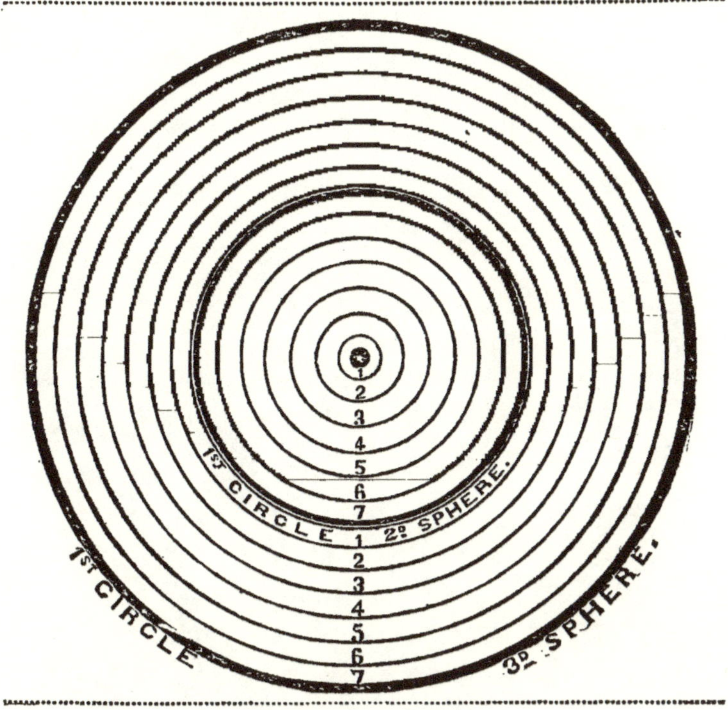

[EXPLANATION.]

1. Wisdom, wholly selfish, or seeking selfish good.
2. Wisdom, controlled by popular opinion.
3. Wisdom, independent of popularity, but not perfect.
4. Wisdom, which seeks others' good and not evil.
5. Wisdom, in purity, or a circle of Purity.
6. Wisdom, in perfection to prophecy.
7. Wisdom, to instruct all others of less wisdom.

CHAPTER I.

SICKNESS, DEATH, AND BURIAL OF THOMAS PAINE.

Conversation with his physician, and his indifference about death—The minister sent for—Prayer—Meditation on life—Age of Reason—A swoon—Sees a spirit—The effort of the spirit to identify herself—His death—Funeral services—Doubting minister—Conversation with his spirit companion—Benediction, and opinions of the people—The end of wonders—Joy in his new sphere—The greeting—The woman and the doctor—His mother—Her welcome—His grave—The thoughts of the grave digger—Anxiety to reveal the truth—Promise to him of a coming time when it could be done with safety to mediums—Origin of sight—Thoughts of minds at his grave—Disclaims intentional wrong—Objections to religion—Visit to the minister—Conversation between the minister and servant—Prayer—Servant complains—Cheering conversation of Paine and his companion—Proposes to relate his experience, and signs his name.

In the progress of mind to the unseen world, there is no wonder within the range of human perception, analagous to the transition of the spirit in what is called death. I will relate the incidents of my experience. For some weeks previous to my exit, my attending physician gave me up as incurable. Still, he continued his visits, and experimented in every possible way his ingenuity and wisdom could devise, to control what he foresaw would terminate in my dissolution. At length, approaching my bedside, he said in a tremulous tone, "I fear you will not live to see the light of morning." "I replied, in a whisper, "I see no one, then, to do what will be required at my demise."

"What do you require?" said the doctor.

"Only that my body be decently interred," I responded.

I saw he felt moved by my indifference, and I requested him to invite the parish minister to make a prayer. He did so. I was still unmoved by his pathetic appeals to Heaven to bless my soul with the outpourings of his grace upon me. I felt no solicitude about my fate. All seemed dark and hopeless, with no ray of light to gladden the soul of a dying unbeliever in revelation. I was willing to see, but no light came to my relief. In this state of awful gloom, when midnight blackness offered no consolation, when the idolatry of monkish mockery gave no satisfaction, and when no ostentatious show of worldly gain or honor wearied my mind with their cares, I said, "what is life?" I answered, "'tis but a dream." "Then what have I done which is not a dream?" I wondered. "There is my Age of Reason, and is that a dream?" I saw no dream in that work. It was a reality. It was my work. I saw it was not a dream. There was what the minister had not disturbed. He did not overthrow what it contained. He prayed against my infidelity, but he did not lessen my convictions in any position I had taken. No: weak and worn out with disease as I was, he made no issue with my attack upon his faith. He went away, and I saw him no more, till no more of flesh and blood imprisoned my spirit. I was well satisfied he was afraid of me. I was never more satisfied of the truth of my book. Still, it was not what I wanted. It did not aid me in my lone chamber of weakness and destitution. It gave me no solace, save the reflection that I had served the cause of human freedom, and had triumphed over the dogmatical assumptions of a miserable theology. I was not wholly satisfied that I was altogether right, but I was very certain that religionists were wrong. I saw the corruption and hypocrisy of those who professed to be Christians, and I was persuaded that what they taught upheld them in their hypocrisy. In this frame of mind, I neither felt wounded by their assaults upon my work, nor was I afraid of what would be my condition after death.

Near the close of my earthly life, I fell into a swoon, and I saw what was more evidence to me of a future life, than all I had ever heard or read. I saw my wisdom isolated, and torn in fragments. There came near me one whom I loved in my youth; one who was dear to me when I was in my years of prime; and who cherished an attachment for me, which even death had no power to dissolve. She had passed away. I had wept over her grave. I had mourned her death as the severest of all possible calamities. We were united. Nothing but the form of marriage was wanting to make us one in the sight of the world. We were married. I loved her as I never loved another. She was my idol; and never was homage more sincere and fervent than that which I gave her; never was my soul so willingly captivated as when I enjoyed her affection. Never was my distress equaled as when I saw her coffined for the grave. Oh, sadness! thou hast no wisdom for the bereaved! From that day to the period above related, I had no music like hers to cheer me onward through the night of my corroded sympathy, nor was there hope that we should meet on the plain of conjugal affinity which we now enjoy.

In that swoon, I saw her as in the bloom of her virgin innocence. She came to me and said, "Thomas! be of good cheer, I am with you."

"Half wise am I to believe in an apparition, or have I lost my reason that I should see a ghost by my bedside?" I wondered to myself.

"Be not deceived. Do you not see me? Here is my hand, and here the ring with my name engraved, and do you not know my voice?" she replied.

"Indeed, your voice I know; I know all; but what are you?" may I ask.

"I am your betrothed, your confiding companion. I have watched over you with more care than you would have deemed necessary, had I been formally united with you in marriage. I have come now as a spirit to remove your doubts, and conduct you to a circle where the weariness of the world will disturb no more."

"A spirit! a spirit!" I said in amazement.

"Yes, a spirit, a spirit you mourned as dead, is with you."

"Is it possible? it is not—no, it is not."

"It is possible. Never question what you know, Thomas."

"I doubt not my senses, but my sight."

"Then take my hand, as you once plighted your love to me, and bear me witness that what you feel is not a delusion, nor my speech a mockery of heaven."

I gave her my warm hand, and never doubted again. But, ere the morning sun had appeared, I passed the portal of death, and saw the neighbors and friends preparing for the funeral. The minister was sent for. He came. With uplifted hands he besought God to comfort the weeping circle; but I saw he had no confidence that his prayer would be answered. He bewailed death as a curse, and mourned that Adam and all his posterity had no hope in heaven, only in Jesus. He opened what he said was the word of God, and read, "There is hope of a tree, if it be cut down, that it will sprout again;" but what is man, that the Almighty should call him to a new sphere, he did not seem to comprehend.

As I stood near him during the whole service, I felt moved to say, "Oh, thou of little faith; wherefore dost thou doubt?" But my companion said, "He will not believe though one go to him from the dead; he has Moses and the prophets, Jesus and the apostles, but will he not dispute their sayings?"

T. Can he dispute what he shall see and hear?

C. And did not *you* doubt me, Thomas? When I spoke, and when you saw me, you said, "It is not possible." Though you saw my hand, and the ring on my finger, you would not admit my presence. Then you said, "I doubt my sight."

T. And will he, a believer in spirits, do the same?

C. He will not deny spirits, neither will he admit what he sees.

T. Why?

C. He will say, as you said, "I doubt my sight."

T. But will a believer in revelation doubt, as I doubted?

C. A believer in revelation doubts, and will doubt, his sight as soon as an unbeliever. Both cavil with the only rule which nature has given them to determine the existence of things, and their relation to each other.

T. Who, then, are believers?

C. "Hath not God concluded all in unbelief, that he might have mercy upon all?" All are unbelievers. The minister does not believe that you and I are present, and hear his speech. He does not believe what we know, that his belief is unbelief of the truth in many things: so is his unbelief a denial of the truth in other things.

The minister concluded his service, and my body was

deposited in the grave. I waited to hear the benediction: "Dust unto dust is the law of nature; but the spirit must appear before the bar of God to receive the penalty of violated law," he said, in mournful solemnity. The circle departed, saying, "he was more charitable than was to be expected. Paine was an infidel, and what could he do less than speak what he believed. He was satisfied that the deceased had no eternal life abiding in him, and it was his duty to warn his neighbors of their danger."

I left them, and said, "How long shall it be to the end of these wonders?"

My companion replied, "The end is not yet. Progressive developments of wisdom will appear, when the dark cloud of superstition shall be removed, so that the light of heaven shall not involve those on whom it falls in the trouble of wicked men. The spirits of this sphere have waited for the coming of that day, and come it will, when opinions shall not triumph over facts, and truth shall not be rejected because it disagrees with the errors of religionists."

But to return to my exit. When my companion gave me her hand, I faintly said, "God be praised," and languished into life. There was no other spirit near me, when I closed my race on earth. I was not without her presence a moment, though a short interval elapsed in which I saw no one. She saw me in my chamber, and she came to conduct me to wisdom which I had not known. As a dear spirit, I loved her; but when I found myself where I could see the body I once bore, and the countenances I was well acquainted with, it was a scene so wholly unexpected, that I was overpowered with joy, and my whole nature suffused with intense gratitude to that divine Being, whose name and mercies I had derided in my weakness and ignorance.

The first object which I saw was my companion. She smiled and said, "Thomas, thou hast passed over the valley; fear no evil; I am with thee." I could see what they were doing with my body, when I was conversing with her.

It was not over an hour after I left it, till my spirit was conscious of all that was passing in the house. I saw the woman, who occupied the house, interested in preserving my features from discoloration, and bathing my mortal casement with wet cloths. She was not well satisfied with the physician. He wanted her to ask the minister to make a prayer, but she refused. He told her it was customary on such occasions to invite the minister to pray. She said "he would soon need something more, and I am not in a condition to pay him for his services." He told her that he would settle all, if she desired. "I will not make a mock of the thing," she replied; "but to tell you the truth, doctor, I do not believe in praying over the dead."

The next wonder, which I was permitted to see, was the spirit of my mother. She was a mother; I was now a spirit, and she came to me, and said: "My son, my child, I call you, my child. The storm of contention has passed. The angry tempest is now gone by. Here, my son, are the realities of happiness. I have labored to make you wise in the wisdom of nature, but alas! I was not successful, only in a degree. I have now an opportunity to conduct you where wisdom will be unfolded in measureless profusion." So saying, she bade me follow her.

In the mean time, my companion stood by my side, and we both instantly obeyed. The angel mother led our way to a grave, which was being dug for my remains. "There," said she, "is the end of all flesh. There is the grave of your dust, and though it shall be deposited in it, your spirit will live forever. Such will be the end of all living. Do you not hear the workman?" I listened, and the thoughts of the poor man came up to my spirit in wonderful sweetness, as he moved the shovel with its load of earth. "Ah!" said he, "there are many who respect the talents of the dead, but few who care for the living."

I saw him as he filled the grave. I heard him say, mentally, "No man liveth and dieth not. I have dug many graves, but where is the man who will not work when human bodies need a burial? Oh! what would I give to know that, when my body is wasted in dust, I shall live in heaven. But, alas! what do I ask? My soul weeps to know what God has refused to mortals."

"Do you see," said my mother, "that nature is true to human good, while ignorance conceals her worth?"

"I see," replied my companion, and we went away.

As we left the grave I was well satisfied that the reflections of the poor man were mournfully true. I was not without misgivings that my Age of Reason sought not to gratify the mind in its hope of immortality. I said, "when will the day come that I can make known the truth, and correct the errors of my work?"

My mother replied, "The world is not yet prepared to hear such news. I will not wrong the truth by an attempt to reveal it."

T. But will not a day come when spirits can unfold to mind in the body the wonders of this sphere?

M. When minds emerge from the darkness of their superstition, and spirits can control, without wrong to the medium, we can make known to them the wonders of this world of life; but, while they are controlled by their superstition, the revealment would subject the medium to severe penal sufferings, and the execration of all who are not controlled by us. The people are more tenacious of their creeds than what is consistent with the safety of such, as will be required to act in a wonderful manner to overcome their errors. I see, that when Jesus came, he was not opposed with more violent measures than religionists are prepared to adopt to suppress whatever contradicts their faith and practice. But there will come a day when spirits can reveal the truth, without involving the medium in trouble at the hands of its enemies, and when the inalienable rights of mind will be protected by the voice of public opinion. Be patient, therefore, my son ; for the coming of that day will change the gloom of the grave into the joy of immortal rest. It will come with wonder, and mind will understand that the tomb is not the home of the soul.

The sun was now sinking behind the western hills. Then I said, "why are midnight and mid-day alike to spirits? Why is not the rudimental sphere developed as mind is here?"

"I see you will wonder, Thomas. Are not the night and the day alike unto God? Does he not make light, and create darkness? Are not light and darkness the result of causes which harmonize in the well being of mind in the body? Must not the spirit, wearied with its load of dust, have hours of repose and rest?"

"Very true," I replied; "but why do they not see as spirits see?"

"Our vision is not as theirs; when we see, it is because

the undulations of light, falling upon us, are unobstructed by other things. You will find light without darkness in your path, because there is more light in spiritual than earthly bodies. Light emanates from particles of matter thrown off from dense globes in straight lines, which coming in collision with each other, produce a concussion in such rapid succession, as to evolve what is called light. The law of what is called the solar system, governs worlds of other systems. A ray diverging from the sun meets a ray from earth, which produces what is called friction among the innumerable particles in their passage from one point to another. This friction emits a blaze from the two particles. These wonders are actually transpiring every instant, within scarcely perceptible distances, so that no darkness can exist when they occur. There is an ocean of rays commingling in their destined course, and forced along their pathway by attractive and repulsive forces in the great economy of nature. Now, it is only the grosser particles, migrating from one globe to another, that make light to the inhabitants of the rudimental sphere, while spirits are able to discover light, or, as I would say, see the friction, or light, emitted by the friction of lesser rays coming in contact with each other. When the sun is visible to minds in the body, rays from it fall in direct lines to earth, and rays from earth pass in direct lines to the sun. When rays pass in direct lines and meet, the concussion or friction is greater than when striking each other obliquely. Hence, the greater the friction, the greater the light. And the nearer to earth the contact of the rays, the more sensible the effect upon the retina of the human eye. This accounts for the darkness called night, and the light called day. At night, the rays, migrating from the sun to earth and earth to sun, must strike each other obliquely, and at a greater distance from the eye of man. But spirits are aided by the friction of infinitely more refined particles of matter meeting the inconceivably more refined particles of earth, occasioned by the influence of other planets upon it. As the attractive and repulsive forces are equal to the density, distance, and magnitude of the several orbs, so are the rays refined; and you will find that the balances are in just proportion throughout the immensity of the Creator's works. We see that refined particles, or rays, more clearly give light to us, than the grosser particles, emitted by stronger attractions, do to minds in grosser organs of sight. Every thing is adapted to its condition. Nothing is unwise in the order of the divine government."

But, when we were at the grave, I saw no mind relieved. "Thomas Paine was an infidel," said they. "He ridiculed the Bible. He was not moral, even. He was addicted to intemperance. He lived with a strange woman. He would not repent, and be converted; and he died without having experienced religion. He must now atone for his conduct."

I wished to say, but wishes were vain, "My wrongs were not wrongs of injury intentional to others. I had erred; and I would, if I could, have atoned for those errors; but my works were not worse than those arrayed against me. I saw no religion worth possessing in the creeds of men. I was not wise, but I could not find wisdom in the doctrines taught by religionists. My desire was law and justice; but neither were commended to my judgment, in the forms and ceremonies of the church. A change of heart was more mystical to me than the mythology of the pagans. A wise man hath said, 'wisdom is mine,' and what he said I was not ashamed to allow: but I was ashamed to allow what I could not explain, so that others could comprehend my meaning. I was not without reverence for good, but what was good gave me some uneasiness to determine. My rules were isolated, and sometimes contradictory. Nevertheless, I would attempt to draw up rules which I thought practicable, and when I saw what was not wise, I was never ashamed to acknowledge it."

During the evening of the day in which my body was interred, I was with my companion and mother, who proposed to visit the house of the parish minister. I wished not to go, for I was well satisfied of his feelings. I was about to say so, when my companion resumed: "We may not refuse crumbs when no more can be had. I see," said she, "he will not pray without wrath or doubting; but it is all we can expect under his condition of mind. He is now waiting to call the family together for prayers."

"Then we will not stay long," I replied.

"No longer than you wish," she rejoined.

It was a still night. As we neared the house, the work of reading a chapter was commenced by the servant of the house. She read, with hurried words, the chapter which was offered her.

"That seems to be an awful lesson of judgment against the unbelieving," said the minister, with a sigh. "Oh! what would Paine give now, if he had made his peace with God? I fear he is lost forever."

"And why do you think so?" said the servant.

"Because he was a very wicked man," said the minister.

"Are not all men wicked," she faintly uttered?

M. Yes: but you know there is a sin unto death, for which even Christians are not permitted to pray.

S. Did Paine commit that sin which is unto death?

M. I fear such will be found the case. He resisted the Holy Ghost. He resisted prayer. He was opposed to religion. Alas! he is beyond the reach of mercy. So saying, he arose, and said, "we will pray."

He was nearly through with a long prayer, when he called upon God to "remember all who remember not thee. Remember, Oh God!" said he, "all who are out of the ark of safety; for we fear thou hast permitted one of thy works to perish forever. Oh, God! spare thy rod, and let not thine anger be kindled against thy enemies. Thou hast mercy for those that love thee, and wilt thou not also have compassion on those who need thy salvation?" When he had concluded, I heard the servant say to herself, "Who is my judge?"

I responded, by a gentle impression on her mind, "He will judge others, but not as he judges himself."

"It is even so," she seemed to answer. "I never was acquainted with Paine," she said, mentally; "but he was never convicted of any very great crimes that I have ever heard; I wish others were as good as he. Then, I should not be scorned because I am poor, and have to work for a living. May be, it is all right, but I can't see it."

My companion rejoined, "Thus it is, and thus it will be, till wisdom shall come from heaven, gentle as the dew, and free as the air, to chase away the ignorance of a deceived world. Never will mind rise up in the vigor of wisdom, till celestial light shall dissipate the wrongs and woes of misguided mind. I have seen the mind of man groaning in despair, and no one to lift the burden from his soul. I will not mock my inferiors, nor envy my superiors; but I will lead you, Thomas, to a fountain where no impurity can be seen, and where you may bathe in water without shore or bound."

"But where do we go?" I inquired.

"We go where the weary find rest, and the conflicting antagonisms of human society disturb no more. We go where the pure will never become vitiated with wrongs, and where rivers of light roll on, refreshing the mind forever. We go where nature is understood, and her laws obeyed. We go where truth is wisdom, and where no mockery of duty answers the call of need. We go where we wish, and when we go, we will not cease to remember that our return will be cheered with music, vibrating in harmony with human redemption from the whirlpool of angry waters. We will not tarry among the wrongs and evils of a mourning world, but we will visit a wonder away from human cares, where order and harmony are appreciated, and spirits concentrate to admire and glorify the Ruler of unnumbered worlds. There is a world you have not seen, a music you have not heard, a joy you have not experienced, where the storm of contention lashes not against its shore, nor the groans of distress reach the borders of my spirit home."

We went in company. But, at every step of our journey, I saw new wonders, which I propose to write, with the consent of this medium, for the instruction and enjoyment of those who must ere long become travelers over the same road, to a wisdom which none but celestial beings enjoy Therefore, wonder not who writes as you read; for my name will be now recorded, as with the pen of a ready writer, by whose hand I am permitted to subscribe myself,

THOMAS PAINE.

CHAPTER II.

INTERVIEW WITH WM. PENN, AND PAINE'S CONVERSION.

Pleased with his new life — Recognition of rudimental associates —Reason why Paine's writings were unpopular — His opposition to revelation considered —Penn makes an effort to show Paine his error, bnt was defeated — Error acknowledged — Strife about opinions condemned — Nature is never contradictory, but just — All wrong induced by ignorance — Remedy for wrongs — Wisdom peaceful —The will of resistance— The principles of nature enforced — Education in wrong the cause of wrong—Non-resistance advocated — Penn takes him to a temple—Enters an arch-door — Initiation into wisdom — Assumes an obligation — A new song is sung — Receives a lesson — Description of the temple — Name recorded —A book opened — Banner unfurled—Words on the banner — Explanation of justice, wisdom, progression, order and harmony —Duties enjoined — Charge of the master — Emblems explained — Master and servant — Freedom of servants — Obedience to nature demanded — Implements of masonry — Proof of masonry— The High Priest instructs — The book opened and read — Interpretations forbidden — Repentant mind — Conducted to the inner court — The white stone — Name changed — Receives a new baptism — An anthem and ode were sung — The temple by whom made, and its pillars — Hears a wail of sorrow, and prepares for a mission.

When I saw the wisdom of my new sphere, I was delighted beyond the capacity of human expression. I was not wholly a stranger in my new life, for I found a great multitude of spirits whom I had known in the body. I saw minds venerable while in the rudimental state. I was well accquainted with George Washington, Benjamin Franklin, Richard Rush, and many others. I saw spirits teaching them lessons of wisdom. Then, I wondered.

"Why wonderest thou," said a friend? "Thou hast not yet seen what thou mayest see, when the clear light of this world of beauty shall remove the darkness from thy vision."

Thomas. And do I not now see more than I can comprehend?

William. Truly, thou seest what thou dost not comprehend, but thou canst comprehend even more, when thy wisdom shall be increased. I was thy senior in life, but thou knowest my history, in the settlement of Pennsylvania.

T. Indeed, this is none other than William Penn — the mind who never drew a sword to gain a victory, or repel an enemy.

W. I am William Penn; I have watched thy course, Thomas, and I have sympathized in thy efforts to rid minds of superstition and priestly rule; but thou seest now that thy labor was not successful, because the wants of nature must be supplied. Hadst thou not attacked what the mind wants — the hope of the soul in a future sphere — thou wouldst not have found more opposers than sympathizers; mind must and will strive to satisfy its own wants. This is nature; and what is nature, thou didst fight against.

T. But my weapons were not malicious.

W. No; thou wast not malicious, but thou didst what thou wouldst not do again, as thou seest now. Thou wouldst not write against revelation, because thou seest that revelation is true to human wants, and is the bread of the soul. Many things thou hast truly said, but what thou hast truly said, will lose its power for good, because it is found in bad company. I sought to make thee know wherein thou didst err; and, on one occasion, when thou hadst written a work on priestcraft, I verily thought I should succeed in my endeavors; but I saw thee take a book from thy library, which turned thy mind from the impression I gave thee.

T. I see my error; but how could I see otherwise than I did, when in the body?

W. Hadst thou, Thomas, studied opinions less, and nature more, thou wouldst have seen that nature never contradicts its own wants. It does not deny itself. What nature wants, nature provides. Human opinions were objectionable to thee, because they conflicted with nature and each other; so with thy works. Thou wouldst battle with others, because their opinions were irreconcilable with nature, and yet thou didst offer thy own, though exposed to the same objection. They saw thy errors, as thou beheld theirs. When wise minds would correct, they should adopt such rules as will not be objectionable when applied to them. I saw thee, as I saw them, striving for mastery. In this sphere, spirits never quarrel. I was more fortunate; my aim was peace, and my success is well known.

T. How will you control, when minds are wilfully ignorant and blind? My wisdom sees only that force must repel force, when individual or national rights are invaded. I will admit that kindness has great power over some minds, but not to overcome the selfishness of despots and tyrants.

W. Thou wilt see, Thomas, that what is nature, is not contradictory. I see that nature is just and true to all. I see that minds are not just and true to nature, because they are improperly cultivated. It is not natural for minds to fight each other. It is inconsistent with nature for one mind to control another, so as to wrong him — wrong both. Nature is well; but the wrong consists in not obeying her voice. No mind is wilfully ignorant or blind. The will is induced, sometimes, by ignorance and blindness. All will of wrong is induced by want of knowledge to perceive the injury it will occasion to the possessor and others. No mind can will what is seen will produce its own unhappiness, because it seeks its own good. To seek unhappiness would be inconsistent with its nature. To do wrong is to seek misery, because wrong induces misery. Ignorance is the father of misery, for it guides the possessor in the path of folly. When national or individual rights are invaded, it can only occur as ignorance misleads the invader. When human duty is not neglected, the invasion can not be made. Thou knowest, Thomas, that nature is good and just. Thou seest a chord of sympathy binding all minds together. This is nature. Teach minds this lesson, so that it shall see its relationship to mind, and it will not invade the rights of others; because such invasion would induce its own misery — a thing the mind must naturally dread. Had the millions which have been expended in war, been applied to the instruction of the ignorant in the philosophy of peace, little necessity would ever have existed to correct error with other errors, among which the wrong of war ranks foremost. The selfishness of despots and tyrants, would not exist under such a state of wisdom.

T. But we must take things as they are, and govern them accordingly.

W. I would not have thee take others as they are not, Thomas; but I would have thee understand, that the wisdom of this sphere is peaceful, and not compulsory. Thou seest no collision of minds, or disturbance among spirits. The government, which controls minds here without force, is a government more perfect than that thy mind justifieth. No spirit can be improved by evil. Evil is repugnant to its nature. Force against force is evil, because mind must harmonize with mind to be happy. The conflict of two minds is a disturbance of nature's law, and whatever is a disturbance of nature's law, is attended with consequences incongenial with happiness.

T. That is true; but when minds are ignorant of the laws of nature, ignorant of the relation of mind to mind, and the essentials of bliss, they will trample on the rights of each other. Under such a condition of things, is it not wise to restrain by force the unwise and brutal?

W. When minds are ignorant, they should be instructed. Nature demands this; and what nature demands, mind has no right to withhold. Indeed, nature disciplines minds who withhold obedience to her laws. Mind tramples on the rights of mind, because it is ignorant; and it is ignorant, because it has not been instructed, or received instruction. It is no difficult task for mind to receive instruction, nor is it unpleasant to give that which has been imparted. I would have thee understand, that this lesson can be taught to mind, ere it will need force to control it. Nature itself would do this work, were it not baffled by cruel and unwholesome precepts. It is false education which disciplines the mind, so as to make coercive measures apparently necessary in thy mind. Mind is educated in wrong by precept and example, and then coerced by another wrong to control it right. It is cultivated in wrong, and then compelled to suffer for the wrong. Better far that all minds were uneducated, than have them educated in wrong. Education in wrong is what most afflicts thee. No mind need stumble for the absence of light. No mind will stumble, unless it walk in darkness. Let them see before they walk, and they will not fall. No force is necessary to control those who see, in order to keep them from falling; neither is force required to prevent invasion of another's rights, under the light of nature. I see nothing which wrongs any mind, where no force is exerted. It is force against force which wounds. The wound is an evil. It is an evil which force against force has no power to overcome. If thou wouldst have others do right, thou shouldst not do wrong thyself. Resist no good to thy friend, or thy enemy; and thy example will not provoke an invasion of thy rights. If he take from thee thy coat, give him thy cloak also; for, in so doing, thy example will lead him to return both, if thy want be greatest. He will soon recognize thee as a giver of good things, and thy gifts will lead him unto repentance. He will not steal from thee because thou givest, and there are none who prefer to steal, when they are supplied by gifts. None will fight, when they have what they desire without it. None will do wrong, when the wrong discloses no advantage. Study right, Thomas, and right will not wrong thee.

T. But will not your precept lead the ignorant to expect forbearance, and abuse your generosity?

W. It will lead mind to acknowledge, that what will do them good is not an evil. It will do more. It will correct the errors into which they have fallen by wrong precepts. It will not make them abuse my generosity, but disabuse themselves of their own wrongs. Thou knowest what was not done, even by barbarians. When I saw the red man, he never lifted his war-axe against me, nor my friends. He knew I would not abuse him, and he could not abuse me. But he could do wrong to others. He could slay them without remorse. Canst thou explain the reason?

T. The reason explains itself. I know you was successful; but was not your success owing to your well regulated treaty stipulations?

W. Undoubtedly, my engagements were honorably fulfilled, as they were honorably made. I would not wrong a mind, and then require that mind to forbear. I would have all do right; and when mind does right, it need fear no evil. Resistance to the injury of another, is not right, and what is not right, would'st thou recommend?

T. No: but when savages invade, or tyrants oppress, I would resist their misrule.

W. Thou hast well said; but how couldst thou resist more effectually, than by acts of generosity and friendship? Resistance with force against force, is encouragement to wrong. It provokes others to do wrong. "Overcome evil with good," is not resisting evil with evil. There is only one way, Thomas, to do good, and make enemies friends. Minds, wishing peace, will find it with less sacrifice in well doing, than in evil doing. All strife has cost even the victor more than he ever obtained. All wisdom, in this sphere, will show thee, what is not appreciated in the rudimental. I see wherein thou hast erred. I will change thy wisdom, that thou mayest sit down in a circle where mercy flows like a cooling stream to refresh the plants of heaven. Come thou with me, and I will do thee good.

He led me where I saw a light exceeding the brightness of a thousand suns. I saw a door opening a magnificent temple, arched as it were, with stones of the most beautiful workmanship, and clear as crystal. When we reached the arch-way, he said:

"Friend: Art thou prepared to do the work required of thee by the Master of this building?"

T. And what is that work I am required to do?

W. Enter upon thy apprenticeship, and obey thy Master.

T. That I will do, in all reasonable commands.

W. But thy reason is not required, till thou art instructed by the Master to reason with wisdom to guide thee

When we had passed the first arch, I was reflecting on my pilgrimage, which was so strange and new, that I felt my soul overcome with the mercy of heaven. But my guide aided me onward. On entering the second arch door, I was hailed by a workman, who said:

"Whence comest thou?"

My guide responded, "From Edom."

WORKMAN. Hast thou brought a stranger with thee?

GUIDE. A stranger has called to serve as an apprentice in thy charge.

W. Hast thou examined the passports, and dost thou know his integrity?

G. I have examined all, and find him worthy of our confidence.

W. Then, wilt thou proceed to the station where wisdom will be unfolded, and his duties and obligations made known.

As we proceeded, an ode was sung by a great multitude. It was unlike any thing I ever heard before. There was a softness, a melody in the strain, that fell upon my mind with angelic loveliness, and I wondered why I was admitted into a society, where all was peace and harmony, and no discord grated the ear of worthy and tried servants, in this sanctuary of heavenly wisdom. As I wondered, I heard a voice saying: "What man hath rejected, that thou hast found. I saw thee a stranger, and took thee in; naked, and clothed thee; sick and in prison, and visited thee. When thou goest hence, bear this lesson in thy mind, that good may come unto thee from the good thou doest unto others of thy fellow servants, who may need thy aid and sympathy." Then, I heard the multitude say, "Amen." "Amen," I responded; and as I spake this word, I found my voice had changed. It fell so sweetly from my lips, that I was surprised at the sound.

My guide then proceeded to instruct me, that this temple was none other than a miniature representation of nature. "It is a building of God," said he, "and here is thy home. Here mayest thou worship, here bring thy gifts, and consecrate thy vows upon the altar of spirit progress, in the eternal realities of knowledge and virtue. Here pour out the oil of consolation for the bereaved, and here serve God by doing good to those who need thy assistance."

I saw my name written in the record of eternal life; and I was rejoiced when my errors were corrected. When I was instructed, I saw my resistance to truth overcome, and when I found how my own wrongs were remedied, I saw how others might be reclaimed.

The temple was inlaid with gold. I saw a mind standing, with elevated wisdom over his head, and at his feet were sitting students of nature, who received instruction from him. In his right hand he held a book, and in his left a banner. The book was opened, and the banner unfurled. "This is not made with hands" said he, "but came from Mount Horeb, where the everlasting covenant was given to the children of the Most High. Advance stranger, and receive the blessing which thou hast refused in thy unbelief."

I stepped forward as if drawn by an attractive power to do what was required, when he placed the book in my hands, and said: "Receive this Revelation with meekness, and make it thy study. Thou hast ridiculed without reading; read now without ridicule. Turn thou not from its light, but when thou readest understand. Seek not thy own interpretation, but let wisdom conduct thee in candor, to add nothing to or take nothing from what thou hast no right, and which is not thy own." The mind then sat down.

I next saw the words on the banner. It was a beautiful banner, filled with gems and devices; and when I saw it, I read the words, "Justice, Wisdom, Progression, Order, and Harmony." Beneath it was written, "They shall beat their swords into ploughshares, and their spears into pruning hooks."

My guide then said, "Understandest thou what thou seest?"

What will you say, I inquired of Justice?

G. Justice is not cruelty, but is doing what benevolence requires. When thou seest a mind whom thou canst aid, and unto whom thou canst render assistance, be it thy friend or a stranger, then be just to the law which makes thee and him companions, and recognizes the deed of mercy as a deed of good to thyself. If he fall by the way side, because he can not see, then take him by thy strength, and bear him where he may rest. Put thy hand upon him gently, and say: "I will not forsake thee till thou canst aid others as I will aid thee." Let him want nothing, and justice to thy needy friend will be satisfied.

T. What is Wisdom?

G. Wisdom is wise. It is wise to relieve want. It is wise to do good. It is wise to understand thyself, to know thy dependence on others, to see the wisdom of God in his works and wonders. It is wise to act, to say, and to wish well toward all mind. It is wise to speak the truth, to utter nothing but the truth, and to oppose nothing which is good. It is wise to love, as we see love begets love. It is wise to learn, because what thou learnest of wisdom will add to thy circle of bliss, and the bliss of others, when they are taught of thee. It is wise to co-operate in harmony with the thousands who saw thee in need, and aided thy welcome within these courts. It is wise to obey the Master of this house; for in so doing great good shall be thy reward, and thou shalt wear a crown which the ignorant may envy, but can not pluck from thy head.

T. What is Progression?

G. Progression is the expansion of thy mind in the wisdom thou mayest receive from instructed minds around thee. When thou doest good, it is wise; and as thou becomest wise, thy wisdom will swell thy mind with the luxury it gives. Thou knowest from what thou hast seen, that according to thy works of well doing, so shall thy measure of bliss be. If thou wouldst do more to benefit those who need, thou must be found faithful unto the instruction thou receivest, and then thou wilt be prepared to discharge thy trust with honor to thy station, and with satisfaction to thyself.

T. What is Order?

G. Order is law. Law is immutable and universal.

When I say, Order is law, I would that thou shouldst understand that it is obedience to law. Disobedience is disorder, and disorder is anarchy. Thou wilt see that nature is obedient unto law. Planets and suns, and systems of suns and worlds, are all obedient to law. The least disturbance might work a disorder, which no mind less than the Creator could possibly control. As thou beholdest order in the natural world, so let it be thy aim to observe order in the society into whose charge thou hast committed thyself.

T. What is Harmony?

G. Harmony is what we mean by social sympathy. It is congenial with order. It is union of minds. It is wisdom in unity of minds. It is sympathy of thoughts and works. It will not divide and distract, convulse or disturb the social enjoyment of the circle now assembled to witness thy progress in the knowledge of the truth. Thou wilt not do or say what will not be upheld and understood by those whose integrity is vouchsafed to defend thee in the cause of social refinement and peace. Hear, now, what thy Master sayeth unto thee from the throne of mercy.

M. Inasmuch, Thomas, as thou hast advanced to this temple with the aid of thy guide, and hast entered the courts of the glorified circle of this sphere, thou mayest ask what seemeth good to thee.

T. Then, I would inquire, why are those words placed on the banner which I see in your hand, and which seems to indicate the end of collision among minds?

M. Thou hast well judged. The sword and the spear will be converted into useful implements of industry, and the banner thou seest wave in glory over the world of mind. Thou wilt not wonder when thou seest the wisdom which thy progress will unfold to thee; for as the sun is true in its relation to the planets revolving around it, so will the prediction thou seest be verified, and nations shall learn war no more. As thou hast been instructed, so shall thy followers be, till wisdom shall unite all minds in harmony, and order save spirits in weakness and ignorance from their disorder and shame. Then will minds see a victory without blood, a harmony without force, a justice without cruelty, and a wisdom without folly.

T. But when shall these sayings come to pass?

M. That is thy work, as it is ours. Thou must know that what is thy work, thou must not require others to tell when it will be completed. According to thy labor and thy skill, so shall the work prosper in thy hands. But if we are negligent, so shall the day be, in advancing upon mind.

The guide then took me by the hand, and said: "Now thou art introduced into this company, it will be thy chief desire to remember the instruction thou hast received, and follow the counsel which thy seniors may impart to thee. Thou seest many things here, and many more will be revealed to thee, so that thy life will not be idle, but will be devoted to the lessons as they will be given thee. I will now introduce thee to a friend, who has a charge to give thee."

Leading me to the right a few paces, he said: "This is the Master whom thou wilt hear; and as thou hearest, so do ye."

M. My son; hear the counsel of a father, and forsake not the law of thy mother. These many years have I presided over this circle, and my children hear my voice.

They revere my advice, and yield me honor by obedience. At my table thou wilt sit, and receive the bread thy mind will need. Here, we welcome thee from the tears and woes thou hast seen, and here shall thy mind be satisfied with the abundance of mercy received and enjoyed by all of us. But, when thou shalt go on thy mission, bear the banner thou seest, and the glory of that banner shall wave over the world with the smile of peace. Thus, thou wilt see thy reward in the work thou wilt perform for the good of mind in need.

When the Master had concluded his charge, my guide said: "No mind can receive instruction without a teacher, and no mind can teach the truth, unless he be taught. If thou wouldst advance, Thomas, in the knowledge of this sphere, thou mayest understand that thou wilt apply thyself with all diligence to the work before thee. And in order to make thee acquainted with thy care, I will proceed to instruct thee in the use of those implements, which are necessary to expedite the work devolving upon thee."

He then took a chisel and mallet, and said: "Some minds are rough, and need thy labor to remove the uneven surface. Take thou this chisel and mallet, and when thou findest a rough stone, which thou seest can be made smooth, then let thy strength be expended upon it, even as we have sought to make thee serviceable in this temple, by removing the roughness of thy mind. As thou seest we have done thee no harm by rendering thee more beautiful, and better adapted to thy position in this edifice; so mayest thou work to render others what we have made thee. But to aid thee in thy labor, thou shouldst take this square and plumb, so that thou mayest try the stone, until it squares with this rule, and works with this line and plumb, when thou wilt see its use in the temple for which thou hast prepared it. I have now given thee thy directions, and trust thou wilt shew thyself a workman, who will be faithful to the trust committed to thy charge. What sayest thou?"

T. Thou wilt find thy servant faithful in all things. But may I know my Master?

G. One is thy Master, but many are thy fellow-servants. He who controls as a father controls his children, by the voice of kindness, is thy Master, and we are his family. Dost thou not know who controlled thee, and made thee obedient? He is thy Master. The mind that controls others, is the Master of those whom it controls, while those who are controlled by him, are servants to obey his will. The Master is as the servant, and the servant as the Master, in the work required of thee. We may not be controlled as slaves are controlled, nor yet as slaves are worked; for our Master is not a tyrant, but a co-worker with us in the good of all. He rules with attraction, as the sun rules the planets. He rules with wisdom, as he has received wisdom. Force has no authority here, only as an attractive principle to hold the workmen in a desired position — a position for which they are fitted.

T. When we serve one another, we are servants, I suppose.

G. We are servants of good to them. But when we serve ourselves by their industry, we serve them as slaves are served. Thou wilt see we are free, and yet servants of many. Dost thou see the eagle perched on that banner?

T. I see. He cries, "Many in one." Many may be one, and one many.

G. Truly, Thomas. Many may not be in one also. Thou hast seen many oppress the few. Thou hast seen the few victorious over the many. I know thy course against tyranny. I saw thee when a stripling, in the cause of freedom, but thou wast not as thou seest now. Here freedom is not oppression by force. No mind will say unto thee, "go, and thou goest; or come, and thou comest;" because it is his will, and not thine. Here, thy Master's will is thy will, and what is thy will that thou doest, as thou art required. When thy Master and thou agree in all that thou doest, thy freedom is what slaves do not enjoy, nor is thy servitude the bondage of slavery.

T. What rule will make him, thou hast called Master, a master over the workmen?

G. The same rule, or law, which controls the material world. As the sun controls the system of orbs that revolve around it by its attractive power, so it masters or controls them; and yet thou seest no inharmony or disturbance, no resistance or oppression from the authority it exercises. It is control, as we would have rule exercised over minds. Nature is free; and what nature justifies, that thou wilt not disapprove.

T. Can I not wrong nature and myself?

G. Thou canst wrong thyself by denying the laws of nature; but thou canst not do what thy mind forbids thee. Nature is denied, when resistance to attractive power is seen. Nature is disobeyed, when oppression denies the freedom which we enjoy. Thou camest to these courts because thou didst desire more wisdom. No force was necessary to bring thee here. No resistance didst thou offer to the pilgrimage thou hast made. Thy will was as free as air, and when thou didst come, it was control which brought thee. Thou wast drawn by affinity, by law of rule and power over thee, so that thy coming was as free as thy will, and thy will was as free as thy coming. Thou wast drawn, and drawn as thy desire sought. When thou seest, as thou wilt see, the harmony of this temple and its just proportions, thou wilt not wonder at its arrangement, nor need instruction to displace thy errors. If thou wouldst be wise, let not thy prepossessions forestall thy judgment.

T. But what must I do with these implements of industry?

G. Take them in thy charge, and with them this compass, to aid thee in thy work. Remember, also, that wherever thou goest, these thy implements shall be a sign of thy masonry, and thy work thy recommendation among thy fellow servants. As thou hast received them at our hands, so use them as not to abuse the purposes for which they were intended.

T. Have I no one to commend me, but these tokens of my profession?

G. These tokens will reveal thy work, which thou hast received, and thy work will not dispute the use of the implements. Thy name will be known wherever thou goest, because thy works will follow thee.

T. When I go hence, unto whom shall I go?

G. Thou wilt go as thou seest need of thee. Thou wilt see need of thee where thy work will adorn the uncomely things with the beauty and usefulness of this sphere of wisdom. Thou wilt reveal with thy skill the hidden beauty of deformity, and develop the intrinsic value of mind, concealed beneath the rubbish of error and wrong. Let thy dexterity and moderation be known by thy works, so that the whole building of God may resound with shouts of joy.

When my guide had aided me thus far, he said: "Now, Thomas, thou wilt turn thy face to the left, and receive a lesson from the High Priest of this temple."

I turned and walked about four or five paces, when he said, "This is the High Priest. He has a message, and will now aid thee in thy duty to those with whom thou wilt henceforth be associated. Listen attentively to what he may say, and let thy mind be opened to the words which he may speak for thy benefit."

As he arose, a mind said to me, "Kneel."

"Why so?" I inquired.

"This is the order when he speaks."

I knelt, and he proceeded: "Thomas, wouldst thou understand more of the mysteries of this company?"

I responded, "What is useful, I would not refuse."

P. Open then the book, and read.

I opened the book, and read: "What man, having an hundred sheep, if he lose one of them, doth not leave the ninety and nine in the pasture, and go after that which is lost, until he find it? And when he hath found it, he layeth it on his shoulders and rejoiceth; and when he hath brought it home, he calleth his neighboring friends, and saith unto them, Rejoice with me; for I have found my sheep which was lost. I say unto you, likewise, that joy shall be in heaven over one sinner that repenteth more than over ninety and nine just persons, who need no repentance?"

P. Thou hast well read thy lesson. Dost thou wish an interpretation? I see thy mind responds, nay. Thou hast well said, nay. I am not here to interpret what thou understandest, neither would I have thee undertake to do what that book forbids thee. Shouldst thou wish for more light, thou wilt not find it without a revealment be made to thee. What is revealed, is well, and what is not revealed, thou wilt not find by any interpretation which thy wisdom may see fit to place on the words of another Thou mayest interpret thy own words, but thou hast no right to disturb the words of another, lest thy interpretation be taken for the wisdom which instructs thee.

T. How then am I to understand this book?

P. Thou wilt understand, thy duty is not of thy own construction of what is required by the just rule thou hast received; for the book will serve thy harmony and peace far better without interpretation, than with it. Thou wilt see that angels do not need minds, who are lower than themselves, to interpret what is above themselves. When thou hast dispossessed thyself of errors forced upon thy mind by education, thou wilt not need a commentary to aid thee in thy duty. Hast thou not read, and dost thou need an explanation of what thou hast read?

T. I need no explanation of that passage.

P. Truly, and when thou wilt read other passages, as thou hast read that, then thou will say of such also, I need no explanation, because thou will be guided by such impressions as will unfold to thee the beauty thou seest in the pasage thou hast read. Thou seest the prediction verified in thy presence. Thou hast repented of thy sins, and thy repentance has brought thee to these courts to receive the joy of well done, good and repentant servant; enter thou into the joy of thy Master, and sit down with us to this banquet of good things.

T. I accept the offering, and trust I shall prove myself

worthy of the society whose kindness is a sufficient protection against the sin of ingratitude. But will any mind go with me on my mission?

P. When thou goest, then thou shalt have company; but obligations are yet to be made known to thee. Thou will not depart until thou hast received thy passports.

T. And from whom may I receive what is lacking?

P. From the mind who has recorded thy works. The guide will now conduct thee to the inner court of this temple where thou wilt receive thy passports, and from thence thou wilt go on thy mission with thy companions, who will aid thee and co-operate with thee in doing good to thy fellow servants whom thou wilt bless with the blessing thou hast received from this visit.

The guide said, "Follow me."

I went. He conducted me to a circle whose countenances glowed with continual brightness, and whose voices were sweeter than the Æolian harp. As I advanced into a large area in the center of a magnificent court, I saw a light streaming from heaven, and a cloud of wisdom broke upon me in ineffable glory. So great was that light, and so dense was that glory, that I was uplifted like a bark on a wave, but not to sink in despair. As I rose, I continued to rise till my soul was willing to view the height and depth of a mercy that never shuns misfortune, or conceals bread from the hungry. "Here rest, Oh, my soul!" I said to myself.

G. Why dost thou rest? Art thou weary with thy progress?

T. I am not weary, friend, but my mind is lost in the grandeur.

G. Thou hast well said. Remember, now, that thy

elevation to this position was not of thyself, but of that cloud of mercy which bore thee, and on whose bosom thou surveyest the prilgrimage thou has made. Thou wilt also remember, that thy servants from whom thou hast received instruction, have uplifted thee by their strength, so that thou mayest see what thou now beholdest. In due time, thou wilt be permitted to see other things.

Stooping down, he gave me a white stone with a new name therein, which, said he, "no man knoweth but he that receiveth it. This is thy passport, and unto whomsoever thou shalt go of thy circle, they shall bid thee welcome; and thou shalt not take with thee scrip, nor purse, nor two coats, for thy garments shall not tarnish, nor thy mind perish, because thou art denied sympathy and friendship."

I received the white stone with the new name therein, and when I saw the name, I wondered at its meaning.

G. Thou needst not wonder, Thomas, for what was thy name in thy infancy, thou canst not bear with thee into these mansions of light and peace. Thou wilt, henceforth, answer to thy new name in this circle of wisdom. Thou wilt now return with me, and when thou returnest, offer this passport to thy Master, who will explain some things to thee why thy name should be changed.

We returned. The cloud of mercy shone as brightly and gloriously when I descended, as when I ascended. I then gave the Master the white stone, when he said: "Thomas was thy name in infancy. In infancy thou didst not remain. Thou hast grown to the stature of a man. When thou wast a child, thou didst speak as a child, and understand as a child; but now thou art become a man, thou shouldst put away childish things. Henceforth; let not thy name be called Thomas Paine; for thou wilt not answer to a name which misrepresents thy true character, since thou hast found favor which has instructed thee to call no mind, 'common or unclean.'"

T. Am I then to be called by a new name?

M. Thou shalt be called by this circle a new name, which thou seest in the white stone thou hast received.

T. And wilt thou read the new name?

M. "Contentment." Such is thy new name, because such is thy condition. Thou hast sought for light and perfection in the degree of this circle, and as thou hast found, so thou art contented with thy finding. Thou wilt not answer to any other name, when thou respondest to the call of thy fellow servants. In thy infancy and childhood, thou didst call mind "common and unclean," but now thou wilt do so no more. Thou hast seen that thy mind was as thy fellows, but wisdom has shown thee that what thou hast denounced as "unclean" in thy works and by thy words, is not as thou hast said. No unclean thing can enter here, because light and purity will cleanse the immortal mind from the impurities of worldly wisdom and ignorance.

T. But should I retain my old name when I converse with other circles?

M. Thou mayest answer, but when thou answerest, let thy signature be without dissimulation. Shouldst thy friend recognize thee by thy infant name, thou mayest respond; but when thou meetest a mind of this circle, thou wilt be hailed by thy new name, and respond to its announcement.

T. Then a new baptism may be necessary. When my infant name was bequeathed, I was baptized. Ought I not now to receive a new baptism?

M. Thou wilt proceed to the High Priest of this circle, who will answer thy question.

The guide conducted me again to the chair of the High Priest, who said:

"I heard thy inquiry, and thou wilt listen to my answer. Thy baptism was not of wisdom, but of water. When thou wast baptized, thy mind was not affected. The outward man only became the subject of purification. Now thou art introduced into this circle, thou wilt be taught to put away childish things, and consecrate thyself to the work of benevolence. To aid thee in thy work, I will impress thy mind with the spirit of this circle; yea, I will baptize thee in a fountain, which comes like a pure river of water from the throne of wisdom. Reach forth, oh, God! from courts of more than mortal glory, the oil of gladness, and let thy servant be washed in the stream of thy mercy." Placing his hand upon my head, he said: "The wisdom of God be upon thee, and give thee peace."

When his hand rested on my head, I saw a stream descending from wisdom's holy court, gentle as the dew of evening, and clear as the mercy of God. It came like water in the rising tide, and overwhelmed my mind with a flood of living light. I saw the stream, and the stream carried away the question of baptism, and left me pure from all doubt of its character.

"Thou understandest," said my guide, "that water baptism is for infancy, while the baptism of wisdom, which thou hast been permitted to receive, is for minds of understanding. This is the baptism of truth. This is the stream of divine grace. This is the water of life. This is the flood which shall never pass away. This is the sea without a shore; and Contentment will receive wages. Contentment is satisfaction with reward; and when thou goest hence, thy reward will be with thee forevermore. Thou wilt now rest with us."

When the guide had ended his saying, there came a song of sweetness. The whole circle joined in one melodious anthem of joy, which was followed by an ode of order. The words were words of sympathy. They touched my feelings. I saw what was my delight, a society where brotherhood was no unmeaning expression. I had found a kindness which no mortal can understand while in the body. I found a society unlike any thing on earth. It was a society, linked in union by an immortal chain. It was a home, where there was bread enough, and to spare. It was a temple not made with hands. It was made by the Grand Master Builder of heaven and earth. Its pillars were holiness and truth, and its "chief corner stone," wisdom without imperfection. I saw what no mind can see, and what no language can express, in this temple. There were emblems of order, emblems of honor, emblems of brotherhood, emblems of wisdom, emblems of peace, emblems of innocence, and emblems of victory.

When my guide saw my mind contemplating these wonders, he said, "Thou wilt bear with thee the impress of these emblems on thy mind, and thou wilt see thy reward in the obedience which will be expected of thee. Soon thou must go with me. The wail of misery invites our aid. Thou wilt do thy pleasure."

T. My pleasure is to do as thou hast said. I will not refuse thy command.

G. No; as it is thy will.

T. As it is thine also.

"As it is of this circle," said the Master.

"Even so, Amen," responded the High Priest.

"Friends, when ye shall return, bring your friend, without money and without price."

CHAPTER III.

THE LANDLORD AND THE COTTAGE MANIAC.

The Cottage—Landlord impressed — Efforts of spirits — Maniac threatens his family — Landlord advises to send for the minister — Wife wants a doctor — Iron moved by a spirit — Nobleman and Mary confounded by the sounds—Attributes the sounds to satan and witches—Becomes agitated—Boasts of English courage—Gives Mary a half crown — Sends for a physician—Maniac grows more ill—Tea and sugar bought—The doctor comes and prescribes—Aid promised—Curate required to pray at his home—The maniac dies—Grief of Mary—Parental counsel at the time of her marriage repeated—Her husband buried—The family taken to the Alms-house—Affecting conversation between the mother and her son—The overseer questions Mary—Oppression of the poor—Voluntary and involuntary servitude explained.

There were works which no mind can comprehend, revolving around our heads, when we left the archway. "I am not a medical mind," said my guide, "but do you hear that groan of distress?"

I replied in the affirmative.

"To the house of need, then will we go," said he.

When we reached the cottage, I saw the mind was frantic with despair.

G. Yea; and thou seest the cause.

T. Truly, but who shall believe our report?

G. Thou wilt not say, but do as thou canst to aid.

This cottage stood near the Thames, and about six miles from London. The mind of the almost distracted man, was writhing in the agony of death. The family of children were weeping beside the mother, who was sitting at a little distance from the couch, on which the invalid rested. I saw no other company present. They were not affluent, but depended upon their industry for subsistence. Near by, lived a lord of the heritage, who rode in livery, and fared sumptuously. He was apprised of the dangerous illness of his servant, and knew the wants of the dependent family. He came not near, but his wife sent a few necessaries by another servant, whom we saw leaving the cottage as we entered.

"There is wretchedness here," said my companion.

T. Truly; but what can we do to mitigate the evil?

W. We can do what we can, and what we can not do, will not be our fault. Thou mayest go to the landlord, and impress his mind to come here speedily.

I went. He was viewing his farm. It was a smiling season. The luxuriant foliage of nature was never more picturesque. The wild birds were chanting their melodious sonnets, and the lowing herds were grazing on the fertile field. When I approached him, he was meditating upon the probable income of his estate. I was not without hope of making an impression favorable to humanity. I was aided by a near relative of the suffering man. We both aimed instantaneously our power to make him feel a sympathy for the distressed. I saw he was impressed with our wish, and he turned around as if to go to the cottage; but as he turned, he said to himself, "Why should I go there; this world is full of misery. There is yonder city; what could I do to remove the ills of that great metropolis?

It is the misfortune of some to be poor, and what is their misfortune is not my fault."

"What can we do?" said my assistant.

"We will still do our duty," I replied. "If you will act as you can to impress his mind with sympathy, I will aid his conscientiousness to go with us."

"Even so," said he.

We continued our work till he said, "On one account, I will go and see him. He has been faithful unto me, in many things, and I will not now be ungrateful for his services." So saying, he went to the cottage. On entering it, he was met by the wife of the frantic man, who said:

"Dear man, I am distracted with trouble. My God! what shall I do? He is insane, and we have to watch him every moment. Last night he was determined to kill me. He said we would not receive religion, and God had commanded him to kill us. Oh! what can we do," she cried, piteously.

"I think I would send for the minister," said he; "it is not possible he can live long in such a state. Perhaps, he might afford him relief by preparing his soul for death."

"Would it not be better to get a doctor, my lord?"

"It is of no use to get a physician now; it is too late: To-morrow will end all his troubles," replied the landlord.

"Oh, dear me!" sighed the wife; "and I would to God it might end mine; but here are our dear children; who will care for them when death has ruined our hopes?"

"Thou hearest that lament," said my associate.

"I hear. Shall we despair? Never, while human woes require our aid. Never, until success attend our efforts," said I.

At my suggestion, my associate made a noise, which attracted the attention of the nobleman, as he was called. It was made by removing a piece of wrought iron, resembling a broken knife, which rested over a window.

"What is that?" said he.

The wife, whose name was Mary, said, "I see nothing."

The same noise was repeated.

"Do you hear that?" said the nobleman.

"Yes; I hear a rattle of the window," replied Mary.

"That was not the window," said he.

Stepping to the window, he placed his hand upon it, and said, "The window is firm, perhaps it was the old iron."

When we saw his attention drawn another way, the sound was again produced.

"It is that iron," said he; "but what moves it?"

"I don't know," said Mary; "it will soon rattle again, perhaps."

It was not long before he wished to hear again that noise. While looking steadily upon it, the iron fell to the floor. "There," said he, "I knew it was the iron. I wonder what done that!" I stood near him, and impressed his mind with the conviction that spirits wrought such things. He was impressed, as we could; and, at length, said he, "if that old iron was not lifeless, I should believe it could move itself."

M. Oh, my worthy lord; do not—I shall be afraid of seeing ghosts, when I am alone.

L. Pshaw; a ghost never made that noise.

M. What then?

It was not more than a second before the iron was uplifted about a foot, and fell on the floor.

"Well: who knows what all this can mean?" said he. "The devil must be amusing himself. I wish he would come, and heal this dying man."

"You do not suppose the devil will do good?" said Mary.

L. No; but, when I was not more than eleven years old, I recollect my mother said, "a good fountain can not send forth bitter water, nor a bitter fountain good water."

When we had aroused his mind on the subject of spirits, we wished to avail something which would be serviceable to the mind, writhing in distress. Accordingly, we worked so as to make a manifestation near the bed. He was now excited, and verily thought these sounds were premonitions of some awful visitation of Providence.

L. It may not be doubted that there is some meaning to these sounds. If I were a believer in witchcraft, I would say that witches had something to do with these noises. Perhaps, it will appear that my days are numbered. If so, will another noise be made?

My associate now responded by a sound, as before. The nobleman was horror-struck. "The devil is in this," said he. "If my days are numbered, will that rattle of the iron be repeated?"

The rattle was heard again. But gathering a little more courage, he said, mentally, "a coward is worse than a traitor. I am an Englishman. Never let it be said, that an Englishman is afraid of ghosts." My guide then impressed his mind to ask, "do you want any thing of me?"

The well known rattle responded.

"Perhaps," said he "it will be well to call the doctor."

"Rattle, rattle," was the response.

"Now, there must be intelligence some where to produce

these noises," said he. "I do not know what may be the result. But do not be alarmed. I will send a man after my physician, and when he comes back, I will return. In the mean time, Mary, you may remember that ghosts never murdered any one. Have you wanted a little tea and sugar for John? It will not do him harm, — and you may take this half crown, and get what it will buy."

The unfortunate man was worse. He had heard what they had said about his dying. In a half conscious state of mind, he said, "Mary, what did he want? He need not be vexed about rent — he will not ask again where I am."

"No, no: He wanted to see you, and he gave me this half crown to get some tea and sugar for you, and besides he has sent for his doctor — all very kind. He is a kind man in sickness. It is not every landlord you know, who would even come to visit a servant in sickness, much less offer them aid; I hope he will get the doctor, and you will get around again."

The little boy was dispatched to a shop, where he bought a half crown in value of tea and sugar. He returned with bounding feet, and said; "Mother, Sam ax me where I got my money to buy tea and sugar."

"Hush, my child! you will disturb your father. He must have rest before the doctor comes."

In about an hour, the landlord and the physician came. The physician was a profound man in the science of medicine, and experienced in his profession. He graduated from the University at Edinburg, in the year 1791. He received his diploma, and was reputed a successful practitioner of medicine in the hospital of London, for many years. As he advanced toward the bedside, or rather couch of the sufferer, he was met by the wild rolling eye of the patient. Taking his hand, he said, "He is somewhat feverish, and there is a degree of inflammation on the brain. I would recommend mustard, applied to the feet, and cold, wet cloths to the neck and forehead. You must not," said he, "agitate his mind about dying; for he wearies himself too much now about his prospects. Let him have some nourishment, as his appetite may crave, when he is sane; but do not urge him to eat or drink any thing. It is possible he may not want any thing, but you will need some one who will aid you to watch with him to-night."

"I will send one of his comrades," said the nobleman.

DOCTOR. Then I will write down the prescription.

L. That will be unnecessary, because he can not read.

D. And can not this woman read?

M. No, sir; my parents were poor, and I was not sent to school.

"It is important," said the doctor "that this prescription be strictly adhered to. The least deviation may prove fatal to his recovery."

"I can remember all," replied Mary.

When the doctor was about to leave, Mary and the nobleman accompanied him to the yard. "She said, "do you think John will get well, doctor?"

D. It is possible; but the chances are against him. The brain is very restless, and besides there is a predisposition to monopolize the entire control of his whole system. I have never known so aggravated a disease to be overcome without the greatest care. If he should live till morning, I will see him again.

M. Would it not be well to ask the curate to pray?

D. The curate will not aid his recovery, and I would recommend that he should not visit you till John is better; but, if you really desire his aid, you will ask him to pray for your husband at home.

M. Not at home!

D. Yes; at home, God will answer, as here.

The landlord and the physician went away. The evening was still, and no comrade came to watch with the suffering patient. The lone night wasted away, until near two o'clock in the morning, when John was released from his mortal body, and we received him, as we had been received.

During the last convulsive throes of agony, his wife besought God, imploringly, to have mercy on his soul. Never went up to heaven a more sincere and fervent supplication for aid, than this dejected and despairing wife offered for the companion of her youth. Alas! what wife could do more, when mind is torn from mind, and no appearance of reuniting again. The whole heart was given to her husband, and he honored the marriage vow with a constant integrity, which made even the cottage to smile with the warm affection of true hearts. "I was well satisfied," said she, "with my poverty, with my union to make me happy; but now, oh, my God! what shall I do? Oh, dear, what can I do in this unfriendly world?" Then she sighed, and sighed from the soul; but her sighs were aggravated by the mournful despondency of her dear children. She was heard to say: "When my father consented to our marriage," he said, "Mary, you must not think this beautiful world is all sunshine and summer. There will come clouds of sorrow, nights of gloom, and days of adversity. You will remember my saying, Mary, when the winter of bereavement howls its angry blast around your dwelling, and no voice of kindness gladdens the solitude of your weary hours. But now you have consented to marry the man you love; be faithful, even unto death."

Such were the silent meditations of a soul, surcharged with grief, as we witnessed at the cottage of a laborer.

Two days afterwards, I saw the body conveyed to the Potter's Field, and the wife and children to the alms-house. During this period, no landlord came near the cottage. The widow mourned without hope, and the three children clung to her with unusual affection. The boy who was the oldest of the children, seemed to realize the calamity. He said:

"Mother, what shall we do now, my dear father is put in the ground?"

"I suppose," she replied, "we shall be separated. Oh, my child, you distress me. You will see your kind father no more. They have buried him in the cold earth."

J. Will he never come home again?

M. No; he can not come back here, James.

J. Will he stay there in the earth, mother?

M. His body will stay there, but his spirit will appear before the bar of God, at the great day of judgment. All will appear before the throne of God to receive their reward; so you must be a good boy, James, that you may go to heaven.

J. Has father gone to heaven?

M. I don't know, my child; he was not a member of any church; but he never wronged any body, as I know of. He will wait till he receives the sentence of God, and then all will know.

J. How long will he wait, mother?

M. I don't know, my son.

J. Where will he wait?

M. You must not ask such questions. The Bible does not tell us any thing about it, and we must not ask for things which are not revealed.

When two days had passed, the wife and children were conveyed to the alms house. The overseer said to Mary:

O. Is your father living?

M. No, sir, he has been dead about three years.

O. Did he leave any property?

M. I was not at home when he died, but I heard he died in the hospital.

O. In what hospital?

M. Well, they called it a hospital, such as they have in the army. I heard my mother say he was wounded, and brought home to England, and he never got well again.

O. At what battle was he wounded?

M. I never knew the place, but it seems to me more like Waterloo than any other name.

During this investigation, my mind was impressed to work a reform. I saw the injustice of oppression in all its naked deformity. The lords of the soil had monopolized all that could afford subsistence by cultivation, and then demanded the service of the landless at their own apprisal. "What better is this," said I to William, "than chattels in slavery?"

W. Thou wilt see a difference. A voluntary servitude is willing bondage, but involuntary service is unwilling subjection to the will of a master. A willing service is the result of conditions; but an unwilling bondage is the result of cruelty. It is oppression without acquiescence, or reward for labor, by contract.

Not receiving a clear solution of my inquiry, I asked, "What is the difference between voluntary and involuntary slavery."

W. Voluntary slavery is to do what is required by a contract. The doer voluntarily assents on condition of receiving a stipulated compensation. Involuntary slavery is to do what the mind would not do unless coerced by compulsory measures. It does not contract to do any thing, but is forced to do what the master requires.

T. But do not the circumstances of the poor in Europe, coerce them to contract for service, which other conditions would not approve?

W. Thou wilt remember, Thomas, that other conditions coerce the master to hire and pay them for their services. The compulsion is, therefore, mutual, and whatever is mutual is equitable. But when a mind is compelled to do service without the assent of the doer, there is no mutual necessity, nor equity in the arrangement.

T. There is no necessity, I trust, then, which would justify the misery that results from the oppression of the poor, in neglecting the means essential for their comfort.

W. Thou hast well judged. Had avarice the wisdom of truth to control its treasures, the folly of oppression would find no habitation among men. But what thou seest is generosity, when compared with the injustice thou wilt behold in thy pilgrimage.

T. Spare me, then, the sight!

W. Hast thou not a heart to do good? And wilt thou shrink from its performance, because the sight is unwelcome?

T. I will not shrink from my duty; for where duty calls, there is my pleasure, my bliss, my heaven.

W. Then, follow me.

CHAPTER IV.

VISIT TO THE CASTLE.

The Castle described—The centurion alarmed—Faith proved by works—Interpretations of the Bible disallowed—Penn called an infidel—Dialogue between the centurion and Penn—Teacher called—Dialogue continued—Theological opinions the cause of strife and wrong—Paine and Penn retire—Conversation between them—Witnesses beheaded—Dialogue between the Teacher and his Master—A wheel within a wheel—Gold and silver the motive power—Attraction of affinities—Fear and hope make slaves—The king's palace—Conversation between Thomas and William—Grand Master instructs Thomas—A new song—Consistency wrong when minds are wrong—Experience the proper test of principles—Some minds serve two masters—Works justify—Repentance is salvation—Departure for the Temple.

He conducted me to a wall. There was no door of entrance. It was made of scorn. I could see through the wall, for there were a great many port holes. I saw a wild circle of minds peeping through these holes, as though suspicious of our encroachment. When we had passed around the fortress, I heard the centurion say, "To arms, to arms." He was a dark mind. He was told by my companion, "We are not enemies, but friends."

C. What hast thou to do here?

W. We have come to aid thee.

C. Hast thou not learned, that we do not admit strangers within these walls.

W. Thou wilt not refuse what we do not ask. We do not ask admission within such walls, but we seek the deliverance of thee and thy fellows.

C. Deliverance! Who art thou that profferest deliverance to the saints under my command?

W. I am thy friend, and the friend of thy companions.

C. How may I know thou art what thou sayest?

W. By my works.

C. Dost thou believe in the Bible?

W. Thou wilt see my faith by my works.

C. Thy works will not save a mind.

W. What then will save?

C. Believe in the Bible.

W. Will a belief in the Bible save without works?

C. A belief in the Bible will lead to good works, and faith and good works will save.

W. Thou hast said, believe in the Bible. Will that belief save?

C. Yes; because it will lead to good works.

W. Does a belief in the Bible lead all who believe to good works only?

C. Thou art an infidel, and yet thou profferest deliverance unto the people of God.

W. Thou wilt not revile when thou obeyest our instruction.

C. But ought not I to call thee by thy true name?

W. Then, thou wouldst not rebuke when it is not thy prerogative to judge. Dost thou remember the record of thy confidence — that thou shouldst not judge, lest thou be judged; for with what measure ye mete unto others, it shall be meted to you again.

C. I will not agree with thee, that because I have said thou wast an infidel, therefore I shall be judged as such before the bar of God.

W. Thou wilt then disagree with thy Bible?

C. Thou wilt allow an explanation of that passage, I suppose?

W. When thou askest me to allow thee to explain, I want thee to understand, that thy explanation is not mine. Thou mayest not explain for me; for possibly thy wisdom may wholly destroy what those, in whom thou believest, have sought to establish. What thou sayest is thy own, and what is thy own, thou shouldst not impute to another. Thou callest us infidels; but we never seek to destroy another's property, as thou hast proposed by thy offer to explain what thou, perchance, hast no authority for doing. Hast thou read the prohibition?

C. What prohibition?

W. Whosoever addeth unto the sayings of the prophecy of this book, God will add unto him the plagues which are written in this book; and whosoever taketh away the sayings, God will take away his part out of the book of life. What is thy explanation but adding or diminishing the record of another?

C. It is all infidelity to talk as thou dost.

W. Thou sayest, then, that the words of the Bible are infidelity?

C. No; but when thou deniest the instrumentalities of revelation, thou savorest the cause of infidelity.

W. What instrumentalities does revelation require to reveal itself?

C. It requires an explanation.

W. Is the explanation a revelation?

C. It is an explanation of dark passages in the Bible.

W. Well, is an explanation of dark passages in the Bible, a revelation from God?

C. No; but it is essential to mind, in order to be saved.

W. Is that essential to mind which does not agree with itself, and contradicts what is revealed?

C. A correct explanation is consistent, and does not contradict itself, or the Bible.

W. But hast thou not contradicted the Bible, and dost thou not recommend an explanation which expressly takes away the whole force of a divine prohibition?

C. No; it gives it a different meaning, that is all.

W. True; and that is what thou art forbidden to do.

C. I will not submit my judgment to the control of infidels. I see that thou wilt persist to aid infidelity.

W. Thou wilt see what thou hast not yet seen, if thou wilt listen to the voice which requires obedience. Thou wilt see thyself as thou never wilt desire to see again.

C. How so? I am not ashamed of the cross of Christ.

W. Thou wilt not obey.

C. I will obey what is just and reasonable, and wouldst thou have me do more?

W. Is the Bible just and reasonable?

C. Truly.

W. But thou wilt not obey that.

C. Then, I am not a Christian.

W. Well, hast thou said. But wilt thou not revile, and wilt thou abide by the instruction of the Bible?

C. I trust my all in that blessed book. When I gave my heart to God, I resolved to live for his glory.

W. And is it for the glory of God to revile thy brother, and deny what revelation and thy vows unto the Lord have made incumbent upon thee to perform?

C. It is not. But who has reviled? Who has denied his vows and revelation?

W. Hast thou need to be informed, that no name is so offensive in thy sight as infidel? And didst thou not use that word to revile thy brother? Is that for the glory of God, which injures thyself and those that hear thee? When thou shalt see thyself, as thy Master seeth thee, then thou wilt not contradict his instruction. Thou wilt not dispute with revelation, because thou dost not comprehend, by reason of thy confinement, the wisdom it discloses. Wouldst thou evacuate this castle?

C. I would consult my teacher, and exercise my reason.

W. Who is thy teacher, and what is thy reason?

C. That thou mayest explain.

W. Thy teacher will not consent to any interference.

C. Thou mayest explain, and I will counsel with him.

W. Better that thou shouldst call him, and I will converse with him before thee.

The mind soon said, "He is here."

W. Thy teacher will explain.

T. This castle is the gate to heaven. No man can gain admission to the sanctuary of wisdom, unless he shall deny the world, and take up the cross.

W. What world must he deny?

T. He must deny all ungodliness, and all worldly-mindedness, and pride. He must deny the world of vanity and pleasure.

W. He must not deny himself pleasure?

T. Yes; he must deny himself the pleasures of sin for a season, that he may inherit eternal life at the day of judgment.

W. Thou wilt not say he must deny himself the pleasure of good?

T. No: but minds must deny what will do them much harm.

W. Will good do minds harm?

T. The good of sin will curse the soul at the day of judgment.

W. Then, wilt thou inform me, why it would not be better to call that good, evil?

T. It is good now to the sinner; but when God comes to make up his jewels, he will separate the chaff from the wheat.

W. Will God gather his jewels together at the judgment day?

T. They will be gathered from one end of heaven to the other.

W. What will he do with them, when he has gathered them together?

T. He will place them at his right hand.

W. Whom will he place on the left hand?

T. The goats.

W. Who are the goats?

T. Infidels and unbelievers.

W. Who are infidels and unbelievers?

T. Those who deny revelation, and disobey God.

W. Then all who deny revelation, and disobey God, are infidels, or unbelievers?

T. Yes.

W. Hast thou never denied revelation, and disobeyed God? Thou wilt not reject what revelation discloses and duty requires, if wisdom be found in thy sayings.

T. I will not say, I have never denied revelation, and I acknowledge I have disobeyed God; but, I trust, I have found favor in his sight, by repentance and faith in the Lord Jesus.

W. Thou mayest find still greater favor, if thou wilt evacuate this castle, and receive the inspiration of nature.

T. The inspiration of nature! What is the inspiration of nature?

W. It is what natural things impress on the mind.

T. How can nature inspire?

W. How can that which is not nature inspire? Hast thou need of what is not nature? When thou askest, how can nature inspire? dost thou not know that mind is nature, and as mind is nature, so nature inspires.

T. Then what is spirit but nature?

W. Thou wilt answer, "what is not wisdom is nature."

T. Truly. That which has no wisdom is nature, and that which has wisdom is spirit.

W. Have thy words a spirit?

T. They are the productions of a spirit.

W. Is not nature the production of a spirit?

T. Yea; and so are all things.

W. Then, if all things be the production of a spirit, nature is the production of a spirit, and, if nature be the production of a spirit, thou seest nature unites to show what the spirit has done. It is the work of the spirit, and what is the work of a spirit is a revelation of its wisdom. Thou seest that the work must reveal the character and skill of the workman. That development, revealed by the work, is the inspiration of nature. It is the voice of God, which inspires his creatures with veneration.

T. But what wilt thou say of the Bible?

W. I will say, it is the production of nature's works. It is the production of spirit, which is manifested in nature. It is what thou seest, the work of mind developed, or revealed, as mind needed. It is not as thou seest in all things. Thou seest as thy mind hast been instructed, and thou hast been instructed by others not wiser than thyself.

T. But is not the Bible the standard of all truth?

W. It is the standard only of its own truth.

T. Must not all other revelation yield to its authority, when contradictory statements appear?

W. Contradictions of nature are not a part of revelation. That which contradicts nature, is not revelation; because nature is a revelation of the wisdom of God. When thou readest thy Bible, dost thou see a contradiction?

T. I have not found any contradiction of my faith.

W. Hast thou found any contradiction of thy practice?

T. I will not answer thy question.

W. Is it not important to practice our faith?

T. It is.

W. Why, then, dost thou refuse to answer my question?

T. Because I will not.

W. But why will you not?

T. Then, thou wouldst claim an exception to my cause.

W. I claim only consistency.

T. Am I inconsistent?

W. When thou wilt answer as thou knowest, thou art consistent; but when thou seest not what is true, thou mayest be inconsistent with truth. Thou wilt not say thou art consistent in all things.

T. Who art thou?

W. I am thy friend.

T. How may I know thee to be my friend?

W. Thou mayest know, when thou shalt disabuse thyself of thy errors. Thou wilt not accuse thy friend, before thou hast seen aught against him.

T. Thou wilt prove what thou hast said. I will not receive a doctrine, until I see what evidence it has for its support.

W. Very well. Hast thou observed thy rule in the formation of thy opinions? Hast thou evidence that thy opinions of the Bible are all true? What evidence hast thou, that stolen waters are sweet, and that there is pleasure in sin? I want all the evidence thou hast to prove that there is any pleasure in doing wrong.

T. Why, you astonish me: The wicked man is not troubled as is the righteous. He will not need to suffer persecution for the cause of religion, and he will take his ease and comfort in sin without reforming. He is as a tree planted by waters, and he takes his fill of iniquity. He fares sumptuously every day; while the devoted Christian has many trials and crosses to endure, and is troubled about his everlasting condition. Morning and evening, he invokes the blessing of God upon his soul.

W. Canst thou tell me, why nature wrongs the righteous? or by what law a wrong mind is made happy, while a right mind suffers so much?

T. The law of God will show thee.

W. Show me what?

T. Show thee that God suffers a great many evils to attend his children, that they may realize the greatness of his mercy and salvation.

W. Thou wilt not answer.

T. I say, that God does not afflict the wicked as he does the righteous.

W. For what reason, and by what law, is this injustice continued?

T. By the law of God, of course.

W. Is that law eternal?

T. Yea.

W. Then, why will not the righteous, as thou callest thyself, eternally suffer, and the wicked escape their wretchedness?

T. That is infidelity. We must make the Bible our standard.

W. Wilt thou say, the Bible contradicts reason?

T. Reason is carnal.

W. How dost thou know?

T. Because the Bible says so.

W. Wilt thou read it for my instruction?

T. I will say, that is the meaning of the passage.

W. How do you know?

T. How do I know any thing?

W. By thy reason.

T. Well, my reason tells me, that is the meaning.

W. Dost thou presume to use carnal reason to interpret the Bible, so as to favor thy views?

T. My reason is not carnal; I have been regenerated by the atonement of Christ.

W. Thou wilt not receive a doctrine without evidence, and dost thou require of me what thou art unwilling to do thyself? How may I know thy reason is any better than mine? How may I know that thou hast spoken only what the living spirit intended by that passage?

T. I see thou wilt cavil with the word of God.

W. Not with the word of God, friend; but with thy saying. How may I know thou art correct?

T. Have I not said, by the standard of the Bible.

W. Thou hast said well; but thou askest another standard, which is thy interpretation by thy reason.

T. Wouldst thou, then, have me lay aside my reason?

W. No; but I would have thee exercise it; and, when

thou offerest thy Bible as the standard, not again offer thy interpretations as a substitute. Besides, thou hast offered a doctrine to thy friend, which is contrary to thy standard.

T. How so?

W. In that thou sayest, there is pleasure in sin. Hast not thou read in thy Bible, that the wicked are like the troubled sea, whose waters cast up mire and dirt; and that there is no peace to them? How sayest thou, then, that the Bible is the standard, and that there is pleasure in sin? How sayest thou, that the good of sin will curse the soul at the day of judgment, when thy Bible tells thee that there is no good in sin, for the way of the transgressor is hard? Thou wilt not say, we are enemies of the Bible, because we justify its sayings in opposition to thy interpretations.

T. Thou wilt not satisfy me, that the wicked are troubled as other men are.

W. Thou wilt not, then, be satisfied with thy standard?

T. Yes; but thou wilt take it altogether, and not in parts.

W. Take it as thou wilt, only take it as it is, without thy interpretation superadded.

T. Why wouldst thou deny interpretation?

W. That is what has made thy castle. That is what has sown dissension among brethren. That is what has filled the earth with bloodshed and strife. That is what has set mind against mind, and embittered soul against soul. That is what makes hirelings of men, who would interpret what is already revealed, and wrongs the uninformed of the knowledge of God and heaven. That is what divides and distracts whole communities and nations, and makes war upon the rights of mind to investigate the truth, and aid thy fellow servants to do what nature and reason imperatively demand.

The castle was then abandoned by us for a season. "In wisdom," said my companion, "are all things made, which are in heaven, and which are on earth."

"But who is wise to understand the wisdom of that castle?" I replied.

W. Thou knowest that contentment is peace. Thou knowest that minds are contented with that which satisfies. When thou wast in darkness, as thou seest thy brethren, when thou hadst no desire to be instructed only to confirm thy own cause, thou didst not wish thyself contradicted by any wisdom disagreeing with thy own.

T. When I was instructed, I was not as they are.

W. True. Thou wast as they are before thou wast instructed. When thou didst see the error of thy ways, thou didst forsake them. But thy brethren do not yet see. They see some things, but there is a veil over their eyes. They see a castle, and they see the things in that castle; but they do not see the things which are not within it.

T. They would see more, were it not for the walls which enclose them.

W. The walls which enclose them, are of their own creation. The elevated spirit never walls itself in by a work of mind. Those walls are not of jasper, but of self-conceit. They are the works of ignorance. When minds indulge the idea, that they know all that is worth possessing, when they flatter themselves that they are wiser than every other mind, is it strange that they should fortify themselves against all invasion of their conceited infallibility?

T. But, when we go to instruct them, it surprises me, that they should resist the facts which are presented to them.

W. It would not surprise thee, peradventure, if thou shouldst inspect more cautiously the influences which operate with them to overcome the truth. Suppose we rise above the wall, and see from above the machinery employed to keep their position secure.

We arose and saw the interior of the castle. "There," said my guide, "now thou canst judge for thyself. What thou seest, thou hast no need that I tell thee.

I saw a cloud of witnesses beheaded* for the sake of religion. I saw a mind declaiming against cruelty, yet urging his companions to fight the battle, as long as life was spared. "Those who oppose us," said he "are enemies of God, and in league with the devil. They must be overcome, or our religion will be destroyed. Better that all who are not of us be slain, than that the cause of religion should be swept away. These heretics should not be allowed to corrupt the minds of the people of God, and the people of God will not allow them to do it without resistance even unto death." When he had concluded his harangue, the Teacher, who had received instruction through the port hole, said, he had just had an interview with a heretic. The heretic had informed him, that no intrusion was contemplated; but he insisted that the people of God contradicted the Bible in their practice. He said that we interpreted the Bible contrary to its express prohibition. I do not agree with all he said, but what to do with his argument, I am not prepared to say. Perhaps the circle can explain the difficulty.

* When one head controls another, the one controlled has been beheaded.

M. This circle will not undertake to explain the objections of infidels. It is sufficient for the circle to resist the works of the devil, and keep itself pure from the heresies, which endanger the salvation of the soul. The circle should warn evil minds of the danger which awaits them, if they do not repent, and get religion; and I can see no way to do it, more effectually, than to treat them with silent contempt.

T. Ought not the circle to obey the Scriptures?

M. They ought to do their duty, and that duty is made plain by its own covenant obligations.

T. How can our covenant obligations contradict the Scriptures?

M. They do not.

T. How do we fulfil our covenant obligations, unless we meet the arguments of heretics?

M. Who has made you a heretic?

T. I wish to know what should be done, when heretics offer the Bible against our views. I am not a heretic.

M. But you recognize their doctrine, else, why ask about our covenant obligations with heretics?

T. I suppose we ought to do something to meet their objections.

M. Well, the way to meet them is not to reply to them.

T. That will not do them any good. They will soon say we are afraid of them.,

M. They will say any thing to encourage infidelity.

T. They will quote Scripture to oppose us.

M. Yes, and so will the devil.

T. Then what must be done?

M. Have I not told you — do nothing — say nothing?

T. Will that remove the wrong of their opposition?

M. The wrong is of their own choice.

T. Is not the right also?

M. That is a heretical notion. I see you have suffered already from your conversation with them.

T. How have I suffered?

M. Why, you would encourage the doctrine of fatalism. Mind is a free agent. When you make the religion of the circle a choice, you would do away with the cross. That is no cross, which you choose.

T. The unconverted will oppose. Is not that bearing the cross?

M. It is; but you know that no mind would choose religion — I will say that no mind would choose a religion under such disadvantages, unless for the crown it will receive when God judges the world. The sceptic will not receive religion, and he must reap his reward.

The mind was so incensed against heretics, that my guide said, "Is it a wonder that they reject the truth? There is another wheel to this machinery."

"What wheel?" said I.

"It is a wheel which moves all other wheels, replied William. He soon took me to a secret place. "There," said he, "do you hear the sound of something falling on that wheel?" I saw, and heard the sound. It seemed to me like gold and silver. I heard a mind say to its comrade, "suppose the gold and silver should cease to fall on that wheel, do you think it would move?"

"The wheel," replied he, "must have weight, or it would cease to revolve; and when that wheel stops, all the rest must stop, for they depend on its motion."

"What," said I, "do you call that main wheel, William?"

W. I call it the wheel of Ruin. I might call it a wheel of Fortune, or rather, as thou wouldst say, the wheel of misfortune; for what is the gain of one, is the loss of the other. There is gain thrown on to the wheel from the current of popularity, but it does not return again to the owner. He will never receive what he has given to the devouring cupidity of the main wheel of all the machinery in this dismal castle. Thou wilt see, that when the weight is withheld, the wheel will assume its just balance, and there remain. When the wheel stops, all the dependent wheels will stop. Therefore, the weights are the moving power of the whole machinery of this castle.

T. Is it not right to remove these weights?

W. These weights will follow the current into which they have been thrown; but when the current is changed, the bark on which they ride will change also its direction.

T. Then, where will the inhabitants of this castle go?

W. They will go where they please, and be free.

T. Would not the freedom of light and love be abused by their emancipation? Would they not run into all manner of excess and crime, if restraint were removed?

W. Thou knowest thy experience. When thou wast admitted into this circle of light and love, didst thou run into excess because of thy freedom? I perceive thou art now even more ready and willing to do thy duty, than when thou wast entangled with the yoke of bondage.

T. Why not, then, summon our companions, and change the channel of that current, which moves the whole machinery.

W. The summons is what will create more opposition. Dost thou not know, that resistance will not overcome resistance. When mind controls mind, other means must be employed than force.

T. That I understand; but when a work is required, workmen are necessary. Wouldst thou not employ workmen to do a good work?

W. I would not employ workmen to do what was not wanted. Thou seest that these minds do not desire a work, which you propose by the summons.

T. They would be grateful, when they saw the work done.

W. They would not let the work be done.

T. Why not?

W. Because they do not see the benefit thereof.

T. Then, may not our companions aid them to see the benefit?

W. Yea; and, when all things are ready, they will not need a summons.

T. Then, who shall get what is lacking in readiness?

W. Time will work what is necessary.

T. That is now.

W. That is ever.

T. When is ever?

W. Ever is now, and hereafter.

T. Then now and hereafter, all things will be in readiness.

W. Yea; and when all things are in readiness, the work will be completed. Thou mayest now, and ever, remember, that when thou shalt visit this castle, no mind will aid thee in what will change the power which controls the main wheel. It will not change itself, because it desires no change. It will not allow others to change it, for the same reason. Thou wilt see the reason. The love of silver and gold is more powerful than thy arguments, or thy reason. The wheel will go with its load to aid, until it is worn out, and there is no material to build another. When the time comes, and come it will, that the wheel is worn out, and the channel drained, because the fountain is exhausted, the work will be completed, and the walls of this castle will not remain.

T. The wretchedness of this bondage must remain, then, until time shall work into disuse the materials of which it is composed. I could hope that day not distant.

W. Thou mayest well hope. The wheel will not be repaired again. There is no material which can be worked into use. The body is not sound, and the branches are withered. The whole heart is sick, and the wheel will not run, when the current is dry, because no fountain remains to supply it.

T. Of what use, then, are efforts to destroy these walls, or change the current which propels the machinery?

W. Thou wilt not suppose proper efforts unavailing, because thy resistance is unsuccessful. There is a distinction between proper and improper means, which may be employed for the benefit of others.

T. What can be more proper, than such means as will control the main wheel?

W. The main wheel is well, as it is. The control of that wheel is not what we seek, but the minds who manage the wheel as it is turned. Thou wilt not wish the wheel ill, but the minds who are controlled by it, good.

T. If the wheel control the minds, dwelling in this castle, how can those minds be controlled without controlling that which controls them?

W. The wheel revolves by weight of other influences. When those influences shall have no weight, the wheel will not move, because it will want power.

T. Then thou wouldst overcome the weight on the wheel. How can weight be less than weight, without a suspension of the law of gravitation?

W. The attraction of all bodies depends upon the relation which they have to each other. Affinities are attracted to each other by a mutual correspondence. Two bodies will unite when they correspond, by the law of mutual affinity. Unlike bodies resist each other. Fire, being unlike water, will not unite in harmony. They are not attracted to each other. Oil and water will not mingle. Pain and pleasure are separate. When, therefore, thou wouldst overcome the gravity of gold and silver on the wheel, thou hast only to control the love of minds, so that the affinity will be overcome. Destroy the love of gold and silver, and the weight is nothing on the wheel of motion. Destroy the motion, and the whole machinery stops.

T. When the motion stops, what will the minds do? Are they to remain without employ?

W. When the wheel is not controlled by the love of money, the wheel will move by other weights, so that indolence will not be a guest.

T. What other influences can control?

W. The weight of fear and favor. The fear of wrath and the hope of deliverance will move the wheel. But the motion will be tremulous and unsteady. Thou hast seen by the words of the centurion and his teacher, that the power is given by fear and hope. Thou wilt see that when minds are moved by these weights, selfishness is consulted. The love of self moves the mind to seek what will avert wrath, and secure favor. It is not the love of goodness which controls the minds of this circle, but the fear of evil. The fear of evil is not goodness.

T. Are not fear and hope essential to minds in this castle, in order to keep them from outbreaking sins?

W. The fear and hope of these minds, are what make them slaves. Their master understands the uses which such motives exert over his servants. Thou wilt see what will astonish thee; and, when thou seest, thou wilt not rejoice, but mourn.

T. Thou wilt not rejoice, but mourn! What will make me mourn?

W. Thou wilt see, shortly.

When we had considered the motives of those who occupied this castle, we next proceeded to a secret work, which was concealed near a large mansion, surrounded with an armed force of minds, ready to execute the mandates of the occupant.

"This is the king's palace," said William.

T. But what king needs such an armed force? Is he a tyrant that he requires aid to protect him from harm?

W. He is not without fear and hope. He fears what the minds may do whom he rules, and he hopes by an armed force to coerce minds into submission to his authority.

T. On what ground does he base such a conclusion?

W. On the ground that other minds are as he is. He knows his own mind is controlled by fear and hope, and he believes others should be. When he judges others, it is by himself. What affects him most powerfully, he supposes will affect his subjects.

T. Is not that a correct rule?

T. It is correct when both conditions are alike; and it is incorrect when otherwise.

But are not all minds controlled by like motives?

W. Assuredly not. Thou knowest that thy mind is

not controlled by gold and silver, or hope and fear. When thou seest a mind controlled by such wheels, thou wilt understand, that they are servants to the master whose control they obey. Therefore, thou seest that what controls others, will have no power over thee. The king errs in supposing that all his subjects are even as he is. The mistake will work the ruin of this castle. When higher motives control the mind, a higher enjoyment will inspire it.

T. I admit, that all circles of mind are not controlled by the same motives, or objects; but, when circles of mind are controlled by hope and fear, ought not hope and fear to be prominently set before them, so as to induce restraint upon serious evils?

W. What ought to be, should be; and what should be, thou shouldst not resist. When mind is controlled by unworthy motives, when selfish considerations induce obedience, slaves can control slaves, and tyrants control tyrants; for, verily, no despotism is more humiliating, and no servitude more severe, than the drudgery of a mind compelled to do service, which is burdensome and oppressive, and in which it has no pleasure or delight. Minds ought to be controlled by wisdom, which seeks the good because it is good. They ought to fear no evil in doing what will make themselves and others happy.

T. That is very true; but, when circles are in a condition which will not appreciate the high motives thou hast presented, ought they not to be controlled by hope and fear, lest they fall into grievous wrong?

W. The hope and fear of their condition will not overcome what is important. They are not as thou wouldst have them, nor will hope and fear change their condition. Two wrongs will not make right. The wrong of ignorance can not be remedied by ignorance. The king fears his subjects, and his subjects fear him. Both are controlled by fear; but their fears do neither party any good. The king hopes submission to his commands, and his subjects hope his commands may not be burdensome. What are hope and fear, then, but motives of selfishness? The king is selfish in requiring submission, and his subjects are selfish in hoping for greater leniency, and less oppressive burdens. They are alike. Both conditions are equal in the scale of wisdom. Thou knowest, Thomas, that no such motives control the infinite Mind. Thou knowest that his gifts are bestowed upon minds, not because he fears or hopes any thing to be taken from, or added to, his happiness. Thou knowest that wisdom, which comes from that Being, must agree with the character of its cause; and thou knowest that all wisdom, which does not seek, without hope or fear, the good of mind, is not of God, but is selfish and wrong. By this rule, thou wilt do thy duty to the needy, not because thou fearest or hopest a compensation for thy service, or thy neglect, but because the needy demand thy aid. When thy aid is not needed, thou canst go on thy way, but when thou seest the mind of thy brother in the bondage of hope and fear, be not angry with him, but take him in thy charge, and open his eyes to see the gifts of God distributed without money and without price; so that his mind may be inspired with the wisdom of the free, and not with the fear of the slave.

T. Thy words are sweeter than honey in the honey-comb, and the law, which thou wouldst recommend is the law of love, uniting the powerful and the weak, the wise and the unwise, the free and the bondman, in one great family of minds, each serving the other and doing what will promote the happiness of the whole without diminishing the enjoyment of any. But minds often act as slaves, who dread the lash of a tyrant. They are submissive, because they are afraid to be otherwise. They wish to do otherwise, but are restrained, as are slaves, through fear. They work in hope, not of doing good, but of receiving what the king has promised. The wisdom of God controls no desire of their minds. Nothing but selfishness vitalizes their minds for active employment.

W. Thou hast not said untruly. The king and his subjects are controlled by the same principle. They are of selfishness. The king loves what he wants, and loves it so well that he denies his subjects even a morsel of his control. However much they may thirst for his power, he loves himself so much better than he does them, that he is constrained to refuse them what he enjoys. This refusal is resistance of others' wish, and when their wish is disregarded, when his subjects are denied what they need, it is no wonder that kings tremble. They know that the power of many, enlisted in a just cause, is stronger than the few, in an unjust oppression. Hence, they tremble with fear, and feel compelled, through fear, to control by force what they can not by reason. They are in a state of suspense every moment, not knowing whose head may be required, nor whose castle may be assaulted by secret works of ruin in their midst.

The mind wondered, when we surveyed the interior of the king's palace. There were the earnings of the poor, and the industry of millions, profusely lavished in every apartment. Gold and silver were worked into almost all the furniture, and the tables were literally covered with riches of wonderful magnificence. "All for what?" said I.

"Because he is king," responded William.

"Because he is a tyrant," I replied.

W. Why must he be a tyrant?

T. Because he suffers the poor to go naked, and the hungry to starve.

W. Is that tyranny?

T. That is oppression, and oppression is tyranny.

W. The tyrant will answer thee, and say, thou receivest thy wages, and, when thou askest more, thou art oppressive.

T. But he will not say, the wages are equal to the necessity?

W. No: but he will say thou didst consent to work for what thou hast agreed; and when thou askest more for thy service than what he stipulated to pay thee, thou art oppressive in thy demands.

T. He will not say, that he is not oppressive when he controls the price of labor, and makes his servants work for a consideration inadequate to supply their wants?

W. No: but he will say, their misfortune is not his fault.

T. Then he will not utter a truth. The misfortune of one is the fault of many, and most wrongs are the fault of all.

W. True. And when the king can see that his luxury is others' poverty, and others' poverty a wrong for which he is responsible, he will not be a king, but only an equal. The wilderness shall blossom, and the fig tree shall bear much fruit, when the mind of the king shall be converted to the clear sunlight of glory, that shines on the outer walls of this castle.

T. I would that the sun might illumine other minds,

now abiding in the gloom of despair. The morning light has scarcely dawned on these terraces. The wail of woe reverberates along the cold walls of scorn, and the moaning night-breeze bewails the sorrows, which rise where the sins of wrong grieve the oppressed of millions. I have wondered why nature has omitted the conversion of the deluded, who pine in weariness over the misery to which they are subject.

W. When nature is not perverted, and minds are not corroded by the abominations of mythological opinions, no conversion from sin will be necessary. It is not the wrongs of nature, but the ignorance of nature, which makes conversion indispensable to higher enjoyment. Thou seest what wretchedness pervades the minds of these self-righteous converts to the ignorance of other days. Thou seest, that they are not content to work without reward. They have no love of righteousness; no real sympathy for each other's woes; no melting compassion for the unfortunate; no soul to do any thing, unless a golden crown of reward is set before them. It is not a very great virtue to love self, or what will contribute only to selfish enjoyment. When mind loves self, it loves what will do self good. Brutes may do even more than this. They love their young. But mind, which works for self alone, is not active without a prospect of success in its object. The wheel is moved by a hope of gain, or fear of loss; and all minds, controlled by such unworthy motives, must be converted, before they can be wise in the wisdom of God. They must receive an illumination of their minds by the light of nature, unfolding wisdom to the immortal soul. Such, therefore, as thou seest in this castle, who are moved only to aid the needy by hope and fear, to do what God and humanity require, because of rewards, are within a wall of ignorance and wretchedness, which demand the active energy of the more devoted to deliver them. Thou seest the king's heart. Thou seest he is deceived. He believes not the truth. He professes the greatest veneration for God, and the utmost confidence for revelation; and yet he will not believe the revelation which we have found, though corroborated by the natural law of progress. His mind is walled in the fortress of self security. He has built a gallows to terrify others like himself, so that they may fear and tremble before him. Thou seest what will save his mind from the conceit of his perverted imagination.

T. I see he needs to be converted.

W. Then what needs to be done, go thou and do.

T. Thou wilt go likewise.

W. That thou knowest.

T. That will not work his conversion, without other aid.

W. Other aid will come, when required. Thou knowest thy companions are waiting at the gate of the temple, to catch the signal. Lift up thy banner, and let the castle walls now bear the words, which will wave in the breeze.

I mounted the walls, and the white flag of peace streamed in the breeze. By my side, stood the angel of light, and near me the angel of truth. As the signal waved in mystery to the inhabitants of the castle, the workmen from the temple came straightway to the banner, and commenced a new song. They brought with them their implements of industry, and their harps, and an instrument of ten strings. They formed a circle on the wall, enclosing the wisdom of the king and his subjects. When the circle was formed, the Grand Master said: "Thou mayest now work; for these stones, which appear so uncomely and unworthy, may be shapen to the condition, which will not mar the temple of God. In thy work, see that thou take nothing for thy labor, and remove nothing which is valuable, from the possession of those on whom thy labor shall be bestowed. Take off the roughness of the surface, and, when thy work is done, bring the work to one who will inspect thy skill, and he will bid thee go on thy way rejoicing; for that which was lost is found, and that which was cast away is returned. Then strike the cymbal, and let a new song awake the slumbering, for the waste places shall rejoice, and the thirsty land shall be inspired with the refreshing rain."

The circle united in a new song, which fell sweetly on the air, and floated on the breeze, like music which none but angels sing. It was soft and sweet, and the gathering minds wondered at the sound.

When we had sung the song, a mind advanced from the castle, and said, "Whence comest this music?"

"From the choir, whose banner waves over thy head," said William.

M. Art thou a friend, and yet thou dost sing a song? Why dost thou sing, when thy mother taught thee that worship was not in song, but in spirit?

W. What my mother said, I do not condemn; but thou must know, that when we sing, we make melody in our hearts; and when we make melody in our hearts, we sing in spirit and truth.

M. But when thou didst worship in thy body, as thy companions would have thee, thou wouldst not sing; neither wouldst thou follow a banner, as thou dost now.

W. Thou wilt not complain, when thou seest a reform in my customs. I was not what I now am. When I saw my error, I was willing to forsake it. Wilt thou do likewise?

M. I am not in favor of new things, till I have tried them.

W. Art thou willing to try them?

M. I am willing, when I can see and know their utility.

W. How canst thou know the utility of a thing, till thou receivest it? when thou wilt know, thou must know for thyself; and when thou wilt know for thyself, thou must take to thy self what thou desirest to know, so that thy experience may teach thee the utility of what thou hast received.

M. Am I not permitted to receive the experience of another?

W. When thou wilt receive the experience of thy friends, thou wilt not have thy own experience. Beside, thou knowest that the experience of thy friends differs. How canst thou decide the difference without thy own experience? When I was in the body, I had not experience in music. Wouldst thou have considered me a competent judge of that which I knew nothing about, by my own experience?

M. I would not receive a wrong to add to my experience.

W. When thou condemnest what thou dost not know, art thou justified in thy condemnation?

M. Not unless it be just.

W. How wilt thou decide what is just without knowledge?

M. How can I decide any thing?

W. By your knowledge of right and wrong.

M. Well, my knowledge decides that mind should be consistent with itself.

W. Is that agreeably to thy experience?

M. It is.

W. Then thy consistency is inconsistency.

M. How so?

W. Thou hast done wrong in thy life?

M. Yea.

W. Then consistency will not change thy wrong. Consistency is agreement; and when thou sayest, I have done wrong, it is inconsistent with wrong to do right. Consistency is to do wrong, because wrong has been done. Wouldst thou recommend consistency with wrong?

M. Nay; but I do not like inconsistency.

W. Inconsistency with what?

M. I do not like a mind that is constantly changing. I know not where to find a mind that is blown about by every wind that blows.

W. The wind bloweth where it listeth; thou hearest the sound thereof, but canst thou tell whence it cometh, or whither it goeth?

M. I see not whence it cometh, nor whither it goeth.

W. Suppose thou art informed that it cometh from the east, when it cometh from the west, would thy information be consistent with thy experience?

M. Nay.

W. When thou askest me what my mother told me, what was thy object?

M. Thy mother told thee what was not wrong.

W. Verily, it was not wrong to her understanding. But my mother will not say, it is right for her, or me, to refuse to sing, now we have experienced the satisfaction it adds to our minds.

M. Then, thou hast changed thy mind?

W. No; *I* have not changed my mind, but my *experience* has changed it. The music which I hear, is a song that I love, and what I love, thou wouldst not refuse, when no mind would be injured by it.

M. But suppose all were to change their minds, and do as thou hast done, what would the world come to?

W. It would come to a wisdom, which thou deniest thyself. It would come to a freedom, which would destroy this castle. It would come to a joy, which would destroy the wretchedness of thy condition.

M. My condition wretched!

W. Thy condition is wretched.

M. How knowest thou that my condition is wretched?

W. By my experience.

M. Wast thou ever within these walls?

W. Truly.

M. When?

W. When I was as thou art. Thou wilt know what walls I have recommended, when thou inquirest why I sought to wear my wide brim, and my drab coat without buttons, as thou seest others. Thou wilt understand, that pure and undefiled wisdom does not consist in what thou sayest, or what thou wearest, but in works of good to the needy. I was what I was, but what I once was, that I am not.

M. Would it not have been better for thee than thy change?

W. Had it not been for the change, I would have been now as thou art; but I saw an error, and I forsook it. Wouldst thou have me do otherwise?

M. Nay; but art thou sure now thou art right?

W. I am sure I am not wrong.

M. How so?

W. Because I am more free, more happy, and less in bondage.

M. Thou talkest strange things. When wast thou in bondage?

W. When I sought righteousness, because of hope and fear.

M. That is not bondage.

W. What, then, is bondage?

M. Subjection to the will of another, who is master over thee.

W. That is right. Thou wilt see I was subject to the control of hope and fear. I was subject to my master, who said, "Do this, or not do that," and who told me what he would do to me, if I disobeyed. Minds are now serving many masters in this castle, through fear of their displeasure.

M. Minds, in this castle, serve many masters? Whom do we serve, but God?

W. Thou servest whomsoever thou obeyest.

M. True: but no mind can serve two masters.

W. Thou shouldst have said, except he hate the one and love the other. When thou doest right, whom dost thou serve?

M. Thou knowest, when a mind does right, it serves God.

W. When thou doest wrong, whom dost thou serve?

M. The devil.

W. Thou hast done good.

M. I trust I have.

W. Hast thou done evil?

M. Alas! Thou knowest, all have sinned.

W. Then, when thou hast done good, thou hast served God, and when thou hast done evil, thou sayest, thou hast served the devil. Are there not two masters whom thou hast served?

M. Thou wilt have it so.

W. And thou wouldst not have me take thy word with distrust?

M. I would not serve two masters.

W. But thou hast, and what thou hast done, others may do. When thou servest God, good cometh unto thee, but when thou doest wrong, evil is in thy path. No mind serveth God without good, and no mind doeth wrong without evil. The service of God is good, because it consists in doing good to thyself, or others; but the service of the devil is evil, because it consists in doing evil to thyself, or others.

M. But when I do good, evil is present with me.

W. When thou doest good, because thou lovest the good of others as thyself, evil will depart from thee, and thy soul will not mourn. But when thou doest good, because thou wouldst please thyself by receiving the money with interest in return, thou mayest well say, "evil is present with me."

M. Thou knowest that thy reproof will apply to an apostle of Jesus Christ.

W. I know that, when thou doest good to others, evil is not present with thee.

M. Then thou wouldst instruct Paul?

W. Nay: but I would instruct thee. Paul says, when he would do good, others prevented him. When others prevented him from doing good, evil was present. Hast thou not seen evil in opposing good to others, when others opposed the good thou wouldst have done?

M. Others will not oppose their own good.

W. Hast thou not opposed the instruction we would give thee?

M. I have not assented to all thou hast taught.

W Have I taught thee else but good?

M. Thou hast taught what thou wilt say is good.

W. Have I taught what thou wilt say is evil?

M. Thou wilt not say it is evil.

W. But what sayest thou?

M. I will say, I will worship God as I have done.

W. Canst thou worship God without fear?

M. I can worship him in my own way.

W. Will thy way be acceptable unto God?

M. I trust it will not be displeasing in his sight.

W. Then, thou canst worship without fear.

M. I can, if I do my duty.

W. What, then, is thy duty?

M. To worship God.

W. How, worship God?

M. By obeying him with all my heart.

W. Hast thou a heart to obey what is unreasonable?

M. His commands are reasonable.

W. What are his commands?

M. He commands us to love him with all our hearts.

W. Is that all?

M. He commands us to love our neighbor.

W. Is that all?

M. He wills that all should repent.

W. Thou hast well replied. Dost thou obey, in all things, his commands?

M. I have not done all that I ought to have done.

W. When dost thou expect to do what thou shouldst have done?

M. Why, thou knowest that mind is imperfect, and God has made an atonement for sin.

W. Has he made an atonement for all sin?

M. He has made ample provision for all who believe.

W. All who believe in what?

M. All who believe in the atonement he has made?

W. Will that belief save thee, or others?

M. I trust it will.

W. Then belief, in an atonement, will save. Has it saved thee, or others, from all sin and wrong?

M. It will save all who believe.

W. How canst thou decide, that what does not save, will save?

M. By the promise which God has made.

W. Where is the promise?

M. In the Bible.

W. Hast thou other promises?

M. Nay.

W. Wilt thou bring me that promise of God?

M. The whole Bible is proof of it.

W. But I ask where, in the Bible, is that promise?

M. The Bible says, repent and believe, and thou shalt be saved.

W. When wilt thou repent?

M. I have repented of my sins, and found forgiveness.

W. Hast thou any sins which thou hast not repented of?

M. Peradventure, I have many.

W. Will the atonement save thee from them?

M. I trust it will.

W. But has it saved thee from them?

M. I will hope for my salvation.

W. On what promise?

M. On the promise of God.

W. Wilt thou read that promise?

M. That which thou askest, is not mine to give.

W. That which thou hast, is thine to give. That which thou hast not, is not thine to give.

M. Thou wilt not say, I can not read such promise.

W. Thou wilt read, when thou canst find it.

M. The whole world may read it.

W. Not till they find it.

M. Then thou deniest such promise?

W. I deny no promise, but thou hast not found it.

M. I will find it.

W. I will wait thy finding.

M. Here is a passage, which favors such promise, "Who shall lay any thing to the charge of God's elect? It is God that justifieth."

W. I will not lay any thing to the charge of God's elect. But will God justify thee, or others, who have not repented?

M. I hope for justification through the blood of the cross.

W. Dost thou hope for justification, while thy sins remain? Thou shouldst not hope for what is wrong.

M. Is it wrong to hope for justification through faith?

W. It is not wrong to hope for justification, when thou hast repented of all thy sins; but thou wilt not find justification in thy wrongs.

M. Then faith will not justify the mind.

W. Faith will not justify without works of good.

M. Will works justify without faith?

W. Works will not justify, unless they are good; and good works will justify.

M. How can they justify without faith?

W. They justify themselves, because they do not contradict each other. They are consistent with good, and in harmony with the law of God. They will justify the mind who acts well, because mind will not work a wrong, when good is done. When mind obeys God, by obeying the law which God has established in the wisdom of nature, he will not be condemned. God will not condemn a mind in opposition to his law. But nature will afford no justification without repentance. In vain is faith without works, because it is dead, and does no one any good.

M. Then, thou wouldst justify the heathen, if they do good?

W. Yea; and not evil.

M. But will not the heathen be justified through faith?

W. When their faith works by love, and purifies their hearts.

M. Suppose it does not work by love.

W. Then, thou mayest suppose it is dead, and will not justify.

M. But when is faith not dead?

W. When it works, when the work is good, and when others feel the benefits thereof.

M. But does not Jesus say, " Thy faith hath made thee whole?"

W. Yea; and thou seest why.

M. Because faith saves.

W. When it works, not otherwise. Thy faith hath not made thee whole, as thou sayest.

M. My faith will, I trust, make me whole.

W. When will thy faith make thee whole?

M. Thou mayest not dispute the Bible.

W. When will thy faith make thee whole?

M. When the atonement is perfected in me.

W. When will the atonement be perfected in thee?

M. The day will come when all shall stand before God. Then all will know who are justified, and who are not.

W. Thou wilt not say, that thou wilt be justified, when thou shalt stand before God, unless thy works are in harmony with the law of God? Neither wilt thou prove that thou dost not even now stand before God. But art thou justified now by faith?

M. I have said, I hope to be justified, when I stand before God, in the judgment.

W. Why dost thou hope, then, for justification?

M. Because I believe.

W. Does thy belief justify thee now?

M. Thou wilt not receive the true faith.

W. Thou wilt not answer, neither wilt thou show how thou canst be justified hereafter, by thy faith, when thy faith doth not now justify thee.

M. How, then, am I to be saved?

W. Thou wilt be saved by repentance. When thou shalt turn from the error of thy ways; when thou shalt no longer excuse thyself for thy neglect to do thy whole duty; when thou shalt see no mind neglected, because of thy indifference, but shalt do unto thy neighbor good, as his mind may need, without letting thy left hand know what thy right hand doeth; when thou shalt no more publish thy own worthiness, nor detract thy neighbor's; when thou shalt have compassion on the poor, and the stranger within thy gates; when thou shalt no more oppress the weak, nor extort from the needy; when thou shalt love all mind, and curse not; when thou shalt know the truth, and have courage to acknowledge it; when thou shalt teach and practice the wisdom of God; then wilt thou find justification through faith, because thy faith will work by love for the good of all mind; and thou wilt stand before God justified, and saved from the ignorance and wrong, from which thou hast long expected deliverance, but found it not.

Then all the circle said, "Amen;" and we departed to the temple, not made with hands.

CHAPTER V.

SECOND VISIT TO THE TEMPLE.

Unity of work — Each receives a penny — Visits another temple — The Master's charge to Thomas — Advice of the chief — Counsel of the commander — Explanation of the helmet, spear, sword with two edges, arrows and bow, sling and pebbles — Trumpet — Directions to revisit the castle.

On arriving at the temple, each mind took its proper position, and Contentment was made wisdom to the workmen. "Thomas," said William, "art thou satisfied with thy journey?"

T. I am satisfied that I am not as others whom we have seen; but I would that they were altogether as we are.

W. Thou wilt now prepare thyself for what thou wilt soon see disclosed to thee. Thou art not as thou wilt be when the more excellent glory shall be unfolded before thee. Take thy work, and bring it before the inspector, that thou mayest receive thy reward; for thou hast borne the banner, and wilt receive thy recompense.

T. Thou wilt not mark the work as mine; for what I have done, thou hast aided me to do with thy fellow servants, our brethren.

W. Thou wilt come with us, and present thy work; for what we have done is thy work, and thou hast done is our work. Our work and thine are one, and thou wilt with us receive each a penny.

T. Then thou mayest give my wages to the poor.

W. Thy wages are thine, and what is thine, thou wilt receive. It will not be as thou hast supposed. Wilt thou bring thy work?

T. Yea; and here it is.

"The work is well," said the Inspector.

W. Take thy work to the second Inspector.

The work was laid before the Inspector, who said, "It is well, but thou shouldst not hew the stone without a line. I will square thy work. It is well with the square."

"Take thy work to the third Inspector," said William.

"Here is my work," said I, advancing toward him.

Ins. Thy work will square itself. Take thy penny.

"Thy reward is well without the penny," said I.

I. Thou wilt receive thy wages, because thou hast not worked thy work by reason of the reward.

T. What wouldst thou have me to do with my wages?

I, Thou wilt serve thy brethren who have need.

T. Perchance, they will not receive the gift.

I. Thou wilt not need what thou hast, but what thou hast not, thou wilt not refuse, till thou shalt have tried it by thy own experience, and found it wanting. Thou wilt now receive a lesson, which will teach thee how thou mayest not use thy wages, and remember that thy wages is what thou wilt now receive, because thou hast been faithful in some things, thou shalt be a ruler in many things.

Taking my arm, the mind said, "come." We were soon in a more magnificent temple than any which I had ever before beheld. There was a great company of minds, who were seated on each side of a spacious hall, adorned with brilliant gems on walls of light; while over our heads were ministering spirits of a generation who shared the glory of the Prince of peace. Directly before me stood superior minds, and behind me a long line of warriors with broken spears and rusty guns without locks. Their arms of warfare trailed in the march, and their countenances betokened that they had won a victory without injury to themselves or others.

"Thou wilt hear a lesson from the throne of mercy," said William. "Advance near thy Teacher, that he may place his hand on thy head."

Advancing to the required position, the mind arose and said, Thomas, thou hast made a good profession in that thou hast been obedient unto the commands of thy master. Thou wilt permit me to place this crown upon thy head. It is not the crown of tyrants, nor of usurpation; but it is a crown of glory, which the Lord of this tabernacle hath desired me to put on thy head. Thou hast worn a crown of thorns, but now thou hast sought and found the pearl of great price, even the wisdom which seeks the good of those who need, without hope of gain or fear of loss; because thou hast loved thy brethren, who have received thy aid, thou mayest wear this crown of glory. See that thou keep thyself in the way of wisdom, that thy crown may grow brighter and brighter with the using, and not tarnish with rust. Thou wilt not work where thy wisdom will be scorned, but thou wilt go with thy companions to a sorrowing and dependent circle, who will receive thy message with gladness. Thou wilt do the meek and the humble what thou canst not the proud and the disdainful. Thou wilt now take with thee this helmet and this spear, and this sword of two edges, and these arrows and bow, and these stones and sling; and thou wilt also take this trumpet, that thou mayest be armed with the armor which thy work requires of thee. And, when thou needest aid, thou wilt sound the trumpet with the sound that I teach thee, so shalt thou not work alone, but thy companions will aid thee, as thou shalt find labor required. Soon thou wilt go on a mission, which will require all thy wisdom to overcome the midnight of darkness that surrounds the wretchedness of minds, led captive by the deceitfulness of ignorance and folly. Be thou prepared to show thyself a workman, that needeth not to be ashamed of thy calling, for in due time thou wilt reap what thou hast sown; because what thou sowest will bring forth an hundred fold to the glory of God and the good of mind. Take with thee thy elder brother, whose counsel thou hast so wisely received, and also thy companion to whom thou art allied by mutual affinities, and we will wait thy summons. Turn now to the right, and let the chief of this tabernacle give thee further advice."

"Thou wilt go on thy mission, my friend, but before thou goest, it is proper that thou shouldst receive some advice, which thou mayest need. The crown which thou wearest will not suffer tarnish, because it is thine. Thou hast not usurped it, nor hast thou deprived others of any right which unto them belongeth. All they ever had, thou hast taken nothing, but what thou hast is a crown, which we give thee for thy glory. This crown is not the crown of a king, but of a ruler. Thou wilt wear it ever in thy warfare, that thy mind may be loved as thou lovest with unabated affection. Thy authority will not be increased by it; but thou wilt shew thyself a ruler, whose counsel will be respected, because wisdom will guide thee. When thou rulest, thou wilt not control as do kings and emperors, but thou wilt exercise thy reason, and thy reason will be respected. This crown is placed on thy head to make known the majesty of truth, which is shielded by it from all harm. No mind can fault a crown, when honored by wisdom in him who wears it. The crown is well; but the abuse of power is not guarantied by this gift. Thou wilt not abuse thy authority by contributing to the welfare of the rich, from the industry of the poor. Such is not the authority conferred on thee by this crown. But thou wilt contribute from the income of the rich, to aid the poor. Those who need will receive thy care, and thou wilt exercise thy wisdom to convince the rich that thy crown should be worn by them. And when they come to lay their gifts before thee, thou wilt say, ' remember the needy," for these words are written on this crown. Thou wilt also say, 'take this crown from my head, when I dishonor it, by refusing to obey its requirements.' Therefore, let these words be true and faithful in thy way, and let thy conduct show that our confidence has not been misplaced. My aid will be given thee in the work of reform. Thou wilt now receive thy lesson from the commander of this temple, who will tell thee what thou wilt do with the warlike implements thou has received from the chief. Proceed to his chair."

Turning to the right, so as to face about, I came before the commander, who addressed me as follows:

"Hast thou been a warrior?"

"I have not assumed to fight with such weapons."

"Thou wilt now assume to fight the good fight of wisdom. The helmet is thy protection against harm. Thou wilt wear it evermore. Thou wilt not use it in mortal combat, for thou hast not enlisted for such service. But thou hast engaged to do thy duty, and where thy duty calls thee to scenes of wrong, this helmet will aid thee to overcome the hostility of contending parties. It will shield thee from the wrongs of the ignorant, and the assaults of the wicked. Thou seest the word written thereon. It is Peace. The peace thou wilt bear in thy bosom, will overcome the resistance of wrong, and war will cease. The helmet will protect; for war never rages where peace reigns. Thou wilt bear the banner and the helmet, and no foe will attack thee, because there will be no resistance offered by thee, save the power which thy example will inspire in the minds who wrangle with each other. Thou wilt first publish thy motives in the camp of the enemy, and when they read thy words, they will say thou art beside thyself, much peace hath made thee insane. But thou wilt say, 'much peace have they who love the law of harmony and happiness.' Thou wilt say, 'this helmet is peace,' and when they shall unite with thee and thy companions, war will end with them. This helmet will not tarnish. The wisdom of God hath made it, and what God hath made, thou wilt wear with honor to thyself, and satisfaction to thy friends.

"This spear is warlike. Thou wilt not war with thy brethren with this weapon. It is given thee for a nobler purpose than the destruction of enemies. It will serve thee in the battle thou wilt fight, because it is not carnal. It is a spear that will touch the hearts of enemies. It will make no wound, but it will heal the wounds which wrongs have made. When the spear enters the hearts of warriors, it will touch a well of sympathy. When the well is found, thou canst strike the spear deep, and it will not harm. Thou wilt so use this weapon as to find the heart, and when the heart is found, the victory is won. The heart must be touched with the spear of love; and, therefore, thou seest the importance of this instrument. Let thy warfare be such as will touch the heart, and when thou shalt find thy weapon unavailing, thou wilt take this sword with two edges, and lop off the dead branches which overshadow thy efforts, and which yield no fruit. When thou hast cut down the dead branches with thy sword, thou wilt take thy spear, and engraft the fruitful olive branch therein. When thou hast done thy work with thy spear and sword, thou wilt see a great reform in the tree, and new branches will put forth, bearing much fruit to the husbandman.

"These arrows and bow will not make thee unfriendly, except thou pervert them to works of injustice to thy brethren. Thou knowest the history of David and Jonathan. When Saul sought the life of David, he was forewarned by an arrow, which Jonathan shot. It was well with David, and well with Jonathan, because they made a covenant with each other to avert wrong. The arrows were united, and being united were strong against resistance. Take these arrows as a sign of the covenant thou hast made with us, that no wrong shall come unto thee without warning; and take also this bow, which is the power of the covenant; and, with it, do thy work as thou hast covenanted to do, in friendship, love, and truth, and hope of mercy will descend without ending upon thee in thy labor.

"Take also this sling and these pebbles; and, when thou goest on thy mission, thou wilt not make war with those that oppose thee. They are given thee for another purpose. Thy soul will need its rest. Thy sling will bring thee rest. Thou wilt take the pebbles, one by one, and when thy opposer shall make war with thee, thou wilt teach him this lesson: That no wisdom is found in pebbles, and thou wilt say to him, 'silver and gold have I none, but such as I have, give I unto thee. take this sling and these pebbles, and when thou art without wrong, cast them at me, for I too, am poor and needy, and what thou doest, do as thy wisdom shall direct.' Then shalt thou find thy sling and pebbles retained by thee, and thy opposer will be thy follower in the great reform of mind. And when thou shalt have need of our aid, blow the trumpet as thou hast been instructed, and thy companions will join thee in the good fight of reforming mind, without blood or treasure.

"Thou wilt now proceed on thy mission, and, when thou shalt aid with thy wisdom the needy, thy work will be thy reward. Hitherto, thou hast been instructed, but now thou wilt be an instructor of others. Thou wilt work thy work of reform, as thou canst. Take what thou needest for thy work, and go to the castle, where thou didst unfurl the banner, and when thou shalt sound the trumpet, thy circle will obey thy summons."

CHAPTER VI.

SECOND VISIT TO THE CASTLE.

The deacon's prayer — Thomas and Mary converse — Dialogue between the deacon and Thomas on rewards, a day of judgment, and the atonement — The deacon converted — Sung the new song — Departure for the temple — The deacon initiated into the mysteries of wisdom, and the secret explained — Thomas and the deacon revisit the castle.

It was an hour of devotion. The castle was ruffled by the storm of darkness. Not a voice betokened harmony, and each worshiper offered his words to God, as a dictator would his commands to his subjects. One mind wanted his brethren to be more faithful, and another desired the conversion of a third to some opinion, which would disgrace the mind who should practice it. At length, we went to a deacon of the most fashionable circle in the castle. He was offering his words to God. "Thou wouldst have been just," said he, "if thou hadst cut us down as cumberers of the ground, and made our bed in hell; but we thank thee, oh God, that thou hast not been strict to mark our iniquities against us, lest our portion should have been as hypocrites and unbelievers."

"Often hast thou not heard that accusation?" said my compauion.

T. I recollect that was often said by many thoughtless religionists, when I was in the body.

M. And dost thou not know that what thou hast seen in the body, thou mayest see now thou art in this sphere, and more clearly; even so, what thou hast heard.

T. I see that death changes no error, which the mind has received. These minds must have been religious, in the first sphere. They are now religious, in words. They tell God he is not just; for, if he had been, he would have placed them with hypocrites and unbelievers. I see they are mistaken. God is just, and I find them with hypocrites and unbelievers. I see they offer words only. They pray to have God do what they ought to have done themselves. They want others to be converted by God, but they do not reform themselves. Do you know the reason?

M. I see that they are blind to their own condition; they are blind to a more exalted principle of holiness. They have done nothing to reform themselves, because they have expended all their strength in words. They have sought to establish their own righteousness, and thou seest that their righteousness is words; and, when they have worked to convert others, they have made only a convert like unto themselves; they have made a convert with words, and with words they will convert others.

T. When they were in the body, how were the needy neglected?

M. As they would be here, were no other help to be found.

T. Thou hast well said, Mary, that they worship only with words. They worship only words. God is not worshiped. They ask in words, but words never work, without deeds, the reform of mind. They desire with words, that God would reform minds; but they never reflect, that reforms are works. Alas! they will not reform themselves, and do works meet for repentance, because they are blind in the conceit of words. Thou seest their great mistake. Not till they shall see that God is not pleased with their words, and words only, will they look for a change in themselves. So long as they seek to establish a religion of words, they will neglect a religion of works. When they shall learn that God is just, and that they have their portion in company with hypocrites and unbelievers, they will not rest in words alone.

M. But thou seest they will not reform, because they are blind. When their blindness shall be removed, they will see something.

T. Truly: They will see themselves, not as they now see, but as God sees them. They will see that repentance must begin with them. They will see that words will not save. They will see that hypocrites will not be cut off because they have no words; neither will unbelievers fail of a recompense on that account. Thou knowest words entice sinners, and sinners use enticing words; but the mind without this castle relies on works of wisdom.

The deacon concluded his invocation, and I said, "What art thou praying for?"

He replied, "I want the wicked to be saved."

T. From what dost thou desire their salvation?

D. From the wrath of God, and the damnation of hell.

T. Dost thou expect that words will serve thy design?

D. Thou knowest that God has commanded all men to pray, and that the fervent prayer of the righteous availeth much.

T. I wish to know, if words will save?

D. Words will find favor with God.

T. Will they cause God to save a wretched mind?

D. They will avail much.

T. With whom?

D. With God.

T. How much will they avail?

D. They will save the soul from perdition.

T. What will save a soul from perdition?

D. The prayer of the righteous.

T. Have thy prayers saved thee?

D. I trust they will save my soul, if I am faithful.

T. Faithful in what?

D. Faithful in my duty.

T. What is thy duty?

D. To obey God.

T. What is obedience to God?

D. Obedience to God is complying with his commands.

T. Hast thou complied with his commands?

D. I would try to do so.

T. Hast thou done as God has commanded thee?

D. I have come short of his glory.

T. Will thy prayers save thee, when thou art not as he commands?

D. I will obey.

T. When?

D. When I pray, I pray for my forgiveness.

T. Dost thou expect God will hear without repentance?

D. I do repent when I pray.

T. What are thy works?

D. I see, you want me to be what you are.

T. Thou wilt not say, I want thee to be as I am, but

as God is; and when thou art as he has required thee to be, thou wilt not refuse thy mind what good thou mayest enjoy. Wilt thou say, that thy prayers will save thee without repentance?

D. Nay.

T. When wilt thou repent, then?

D. What dost thou mean by repentance?

T. I mean that reform which will save thee from the wretchedness of this confinement in walls.

D. Am I wretched? Nay.

T. Thou wilt not so reply, when thy deliverance is accomplished.

D. Deliverance from what?

T. From thy wrongs and errors, thy sins and sorrows.

D. Verily, thou art confident. Who gave thee power to work in God's name?

T. I will work as my master has commanded.

D. Who is thy master?

T. The mind who controls me and others.

D. Am I not a mind who controls others?

T. Thou controlest thy inferiors, not thy superiors.

D. Thou mayest do the same.

T. Not as thou hast done.

D. Why not?

T. Because thou controlest by fear and hope. Thou rulest as do tyrants and kings. Thy ways are cruel and oppressive, unjust and wrong.

D. Thou wilt not accuse me, when thou art wrong.

T. When thy ways are opposed to the commands of God, am I wrong to inform thee?

D. Nay; but thou wilt not be wrong, when thou art converted.

T. Converted to what?

D. Converted to the religion of the Bible.

T. Wherein do I need conversion to the religion of the Bible?

D. In refusing to join with us.

T. Is that the only reason?

D. It is one which makes thy conversion necessary.

T. Why necessary?

D. Thou knowest thou art not a believer in the Bible

T. Thou wilt not convert me without the Bible.

D. What! not convert thee without the Bible? How sayest thou that the Bible is thy guide?

T. I say, thou wilt not convert me without the Bible.

D. May I hope to conveit thee with it?

T. Thou mayest not hope for conversion to thy views.

D. What views may I hope to convert thee to?

T. Such as are true and practical, wise and good.

D. When wilt thou come to me for instruction?

T. When thou canst instruct me.

D. Thou art not a believer in religion.

T, Thou canst tell by my works.

D. Thy works will not wrong any one.

T. Wilt thou not wrong any one?

D. Not intentionally.

T. Wilt thou justify an unintentional wrong?

D. Nay.

T. Then thou shouldst reform.

D. Why?

T. Because thou doest many unintentional wrongs.

D. Thy charge will not satisfy me of wrong.

T. When thou seest thy brother in need, hast thou aided him? When thou seest him disconsolate, hast thou cheered him? When thou hast found him naked of wisdom, hast thou clothed him with garments of salvation? When thou hast found him an hungered and thirsting after righteousness, hast thou fed him with the bread of heaven, and given him the water of life?

D. That has been my desire.

T. Have thy desires been operative to the good of mind?

D. I would they had been more so.

T. Then thou shouldst put away thy craft, and leave thy habitation of darkness. Thou wilt not do as thy soul desireth, so long as thou remainest imprisoned within the walls of this castle. I see thy intentions are well, but thy wisdom is selfish. When thou shalt relinquish thy wrongs, and no longer wrong others by the inculcation of thy errors, then thou wilt reform the abuses of thy brethren, without money and without price.

D. I would reform any wrong that I may have, but I would first know the wrong.

T. Thou wilt, then, understand what thy wrongs are?

D. Truly.

T. Thy wrongs are the wrongs of others. When thou wouldst forsake thy wrongs, because thou hast seen them, thy brethren offer thee a bribe to refuse a reform. They say to thee, "What good will this new doctrine do? what will those gain who embrace it? and what will they lose that defend it?" Thou hast been warned by awful penalties not to forsake the wrongs thou hast cherished from thy childhood.

D. I acknowledge that I have my fears.

T. Thou wilt acknowledge that thy fears do thee no good, when they make thee miserable.

D. They sometimes make me unhappy.

T. When they make thee unhappy, they are unprofitable. No good thing ever made thee so. That which makes thee unhappy, is a wrong to thee; and when thou shalt put away that wrong, thy unhappiness will cease; but so long as thou shalt cherish the wrong, thy mind will be disturbed by it. This is the law of God in nature. Wouldst thou obey that law?

D. I would obey God.

T. Thou wouldst obey God by obeying his law?

D. I would not disobey his law.

T. Dost thou not see, that it is the law of God, which works thy unhappiness? Dost thou not know, that nothing can be true and right which makes thee unhappy?

D. I see, that when I do wrong, I want what I have not got. I want something which will make me more happy. But it is not wrong to want what I have not got.

T. Thy wants are well; but not thy wrongs to satisfy thy wants. Thy wants are misdirected; they work harm to thy mind. It will not be so, when thou understandest the law which should govern thee. Thou wilt not reform, nor leave this castle, till thou seest that all good is obedience, and all evil is disobedience to the law of God. So long as thou shalt remain subject to the wisdom of those who instruct thee to do wrong, that good may come to thee, thou wilt not refrain from thy wrongs. Thy errors are thy wrongs; and, if thou wouldst be saved from their curse, thou shouldst cast them away.

D. That would I do, when I have found the wrong. But I see no error in my faith.

T. Thy faith is not well when wrong.

D. Yea; but wherein is it wrong?

T. I heard thee say, that God was not just. If God be not just, who will not be like him when arrested for judgment? Thou seest that thy accusation is wrong; and thy wrong hath disturbed thy quiet. When wilt thou reform of thy wrong, if thy God be unjust?

D. But when I said he was unjust, I meant that he was so merciful, as not to punish the wicked as their sins deserve; not that he was an unjust God.

T. Thou wilt not put new wine into old bottles, lest it foment and break the bottles, and the wine be lost. Thou hast made the rent no better. If God will not give the wicked what they deserve, he is unjust, and is not faithful to his promise. Besides, how can the wicked separate themselves from the evil of a violated law? When the law is disregarded, a wrong is done; and, when a wrong is done, the evil is committed. The evil is the wrong. The wrong is what disturbs thee, and what disturbs thee is thy reward. Thy reward is the judgment of God, executed in thy mind, because thy wisdom needs improvement.

D. Thou wilt not say, the wrong is the reward.

T. The wrong is the evil, and the evil is what thou shouldst abandon for thy good; because what is evil to thee, thou shouldst not pursue. The law which rewards thee, is eternal, and, while wrong is cherished, the reward is thine. What is thine, thou wilt receive, for it is just.

D. Thou wilt not say, the wrong is the reward.

T. I will say, the wrong and the reward are inseparable.

D. Then where is the necessity for a day of judgment?

T. The necessity is nature's law; but thy views are wrong.

D. They are what the Scriptures teach.

T. Thou hast not read the Scriptures without thy wisdom to aid thee. Thy wisdom is not the wisdom of God.

D. Wherein do they differ?

T. Thy wisdom is the wisdom of minds like thee; those who are like thee, are no wiser than thyself. Those who are no wiser than thyself, can not instruct thee. They agree with thee, and thou seest only what thy wisdom has unfolded to thee. And when thou hast read the Scriptures, thou hast understood as thy wisdom corrected the Bible. It is thy misfortune to read with thy education to correct the reading, and make it conform to thy errors.

D. Thou wilt not say, there is no judgment.

T. I say, law is eternal, and when wrong is done, a law is violated. When a law is disobeyed, the disobedience is wrong, and the wrong disturbs the doer. This disturbance of law is sure to be attended with the evil which wrong brings. That evil is the judgment of God. I know no other judgment.

D. Thou knowest the Scriptures teach another judgment.

T. I know not what thou affirmest.

D. The Bible speaks of a judgment.

T. So do I.

D. The Bible says, God will judge the world.

T. So do I.

D. When will he judge the world?

T. When the world do wrong, and when they do right.

D. That is always.

T. Truly.

D. Then God judges all minds when they do wrong, and when they do right?

T. Yea.

D. How can he judge those who do right?

T. As he does those who do wrong — by his eternal law. But wrong is judged as an evil, and right as a good. Hence, the mind that does wrong, is judged as wrong; and the mind that does right, is judged as right.

D. How can there be, then, a day of judgment?

T. The day of judgment is when God judges by his law, and not till his judgment is withheld, will that day end. I know of no end to his judgment, nor to the period in which he judges. His judgment is just, and his justice endureth forever.

D. When will the wicked be judged?

T. When they are wicked. No mind can do wrong, without receiving a just recompense of reward.

D. Of what benefit, then, is the atonement of Christ?

T. Thy wisdom will be increased, when thou shalt see the atonement in thyself, and not hope for it because another has it.

D. I do not understand thy meaning.

T. When thou shalt agree with thy Bible, in regard to the atonement, then thou wilt find the atonement in thy works, as thou seest it now in Christ.

D. This is more perplexing to me still. What dost thou mean by atonement in me?

T. I mean the works which Christ done for the good of the needy. He gave sight to the blind, hearing to the deaf, health to the sick, and wisdom to the foolish.

D. Dost thou say, miracles can be done by me?

T. Thou canst do as thy Master hath said. If thou

wilt follow him, thou mayest lay hands on the sick, and they shall recover; thou canst take deadly serpents in thy hands, and they shall not harm thee; thou canst drink poison, and it shall not injure thee; thou canst wait on the suffering, and the Lord thy God will bless thee.

D. Then thou sayest, I am not a follower of Christ?

T. Thy works testify of thee.

D. Do they testify, that I am not a follower of Christ?

T. If thou wast his disciple, his works would follow thee.

D. Then, I am not his disciple.

T. So thou sayest. But wouldst thou be?

D. I would be ever as my Master.

T. Listen then to thy Master's instruction.

D. What instruction?

T. Such as I have, give I unto thee. Visit the sick, those in prison, those in need; and let thy mind be passive to the influence of those who would aid thee to be wise, and the glory of God will deliver thee from thy darkness, and make thee a light to them that dwell with thee in this castle of vain and empty words without deeds.

D. Dost thou say, that I can do miracles?

T. Thou canst do as thy Master hath required thee, and, when thou doest, thy works will testify that a miracle hath been wrought by thee. Thy companions will say, thou hast a devil.

D. If I could believe thy saying, I would follow thee.

T. Thou canst follow thy Master, and my saying will be verified by thy works. The atonement will be in thee to do the will of thy Master.

D. Then all may atone for their sins.

T. All may do good to those in need, and when they

obey the law of God which requires good to be done, the atonement is in them who obey. It is an agreement with Christ to put away sin by personal sacrifice upon the altar of sympathizing humanity. Doing good is atonement, because it is agreement with the law of God, and puts wrong away.

D. Then, there was no need of a Savior.

T. Not so: had there been no wrong, there would have been no Savior; but, where wrong is, there is a need to be saved from the wrong. Thy Savior came where wrongs existed, and where great injuries were practiced; and thou seest he saved many from their errors and wrongs. Thou shouldst obey, and do likewise; and, when thou shalt do as thy Master hath done, thou wilt save many. According to thy wisdom and thy diligence, so shall thy reward be.

D. But, when I obey, do I not then make atonement for sins?

T. When thou obeyest, thou doest well, but thou wilt not obey without a cause. Thy obedience is caused by thy wisdom, and thy wisdom is increased by instruction, so that thy salvation is caused by those who instruct thee in wisdom.

D. Then I have as many Saviors as I have instructors.

T. I would not contradict thee; but still thou shouldst understand that all wisdom is of God. Thy God is thy Savior, and he saves thee in harmony with his law of developing and making wise thy mind. He saves thee only as thou becomest wise, and he makes thee wise through the mediums who are competent to instruct thee in his wisdom. As many as are employed in unfolding to minds the wisdom of God, are saviors to those whom they instruct and make wise. Thou mayest be the savior of many when thou receivest wisdom to instruct others. Thou wilt not save without wisdom; for it is by wisdom that I come to thee with a message which will open the gates of a celestial circle, who wish thy deliverance.

D. Thy pretensions stagger me. If thou art what thy words signify, thou canst do thy will, and make me what thou desirest.

T. I will then invite thee to a circle without these walls. Wilt thou go with me?

D. I will go, my friend.

T. When thou shalt arrive at the arch-way of a temple, not made with hands, thou wilt wait till I announce thy coming. Then, we will proceed into a court, where thou wilt hear and see many things. Let thy mind be calm, and thy vows be faithfully observed. Thou wilt not return to this castle for the purpose of carrying away with thee thy creed, or thy forms of worship. In the temple, we worship God, not with words alone, but with works of good. Thou wilt love thy brethren, and no hate can disturb thy mind. Thou wilt serve God by doing good to those that need; for thou knowest that God hath no dependence of aid from us; but he requireth us to obey him. Thy obedience will do thee good, as it will others on whom thy labors shall be bestowed. Art thou ready?

D. I am ready.

T. Then come with me.

My companion said, "Let us sing the new song."

We stood on the walls and sung the song of jubilee; for mind which was imprisoned was released. Then we departed for the temple.

On reaching the temple, my companion said, "Seest

thou this temple of the living God? Thou wilt wait with me, while Thomas shall announce thy willingness to enter the courts of the redeemed."

I entered the temple, and was hailed by the Master, "What hast thou brought with thee?"

T. The deacon, who has listened to my wisdom, and desirest instruction in the mysteries of thy work, wishes admission within this court, and instruction in ways he has not known.

M. Hast thou instructed him, as most necessary to his improvement, before entering this circle?

T. I have said that which was necessary, and find him prepared to receive the lessons which appertain to his progress.

M. Then thou wilt bid him welcome.

I returned. When I returned, he said, "This is a secret society, I suppose."

T. The wisdom of this circle, who work in this temple, is not a secret to those who have received it.

D. Why dost thou keep thy wisdom a secret?

T. Because all wisdom is a secret to the uninformed. Thou wilt understand that this circle withholds no good thing from those who need, but even those who need, are not always prepared to receive our aid. The secret will not harm thee, neither will it do good to those who refuse to comply with its requirements. The secret is a secret only, because minds know it not, and have resolved not to receive the wisdom which their condition requires to make them skillful workmen in the temple. Art thou prepared to enter with me, and do the work which may be required of thee for the good of mind?

D. I am ready to do justly, love mercy, and walk humbly, in the path of righteousness.

T. Thou wilt remember the poor and thy vows.

D. The needy thou hast with thee.

T. Thou wilt soon become rich.

The same instruction was imparted to the deacon, which I received on my first visit to the temple. When the lessons had been repeated to him, I inquired, "Welcome, wilt thou now revisit the castle with me, that we may aid our brethren to see the light thou hast beheld?"

D. Thou wilt not expect that I would refuse to aid them. We returned.

CHAPTER VII.

THIRD VISIT TO THE CASTLE.

The wonder in the castle—Dialogue between the chief, the deacon, and Thomas—The senior consulted—The circle of the temple summoned by the trumpet—Conversation between the Commander of the temple and the senior of the castle on war—On rights—The conversion of 24 elders, and 144,000—The Commander conducts them to the temple, where they were initiated into that degree of wisdom.

WHEN we reached the castle, there was great wonder and astonishment, that the deacon should have departed from it. I heard the chief say, "I have been suspicious of him ever since the conversation between the centurion and the strangers through the port holes. I saw," said he, "that he listened quite too attentively to the conversation; for it is not possible for any mind to resist the arguments which that circle brings. But alas! there is great danger of their sentiments; there is such a sweetness in their conversation, that it is no wonder that they draw minds away from the truth."

"Wouldst thou taste that sweetness?" said the deacon.

C. I would not jeopardize the eternal interests of my soul.

D. Then thou shouldst abandon that castle, as I have done.

C. Art thou my judge?

D. I judge no mind, but I know thy condition.

C. My condition, I hope, is well.

D. Whereon doth thy hope rest?

C. On the rock of eternal truth.

D. What is truth?

C. The truth is not what thou wouldst teach in thy apostacy.

I said, "Wilt thou answer the question? We wish to know what is truth"

C. Dost thou wish to relieve thy new convert?

T. I wish thee to tell us, if thou canst, what is truth?

C. I will not say, that works are the truths of God.

T. Wilt thou say, that they are not the truths of God?

C. Yea.

T. Then, what is nature, but the work of God?

C. Nature is a work of God.

T. Is nature a true work of God?

C. It is.

T. Then the true work of God is nature, and as thou sayest it is a true work, it is a truth of God. That which is true, is a truth; and that which is false, is not true. The truth of nature is a work of God. The wisdom of nature is the wisdom of God.

C. But there is a wisdom which is not of nature.

T. Wilt thou teach me that wisdom?

C. It is the wisdom of the Bible.

T. What wisdom is not of nature?

C. The Bible.

T. The Bible is not wisdom, but a revelation of wisdom.

C. The Bible is full of wisdom.

T. The Bible is full of the wisdom of nature, which is God's work.

C. The Bible teaches us wisdom.

T. It reveals wisdom.

C. The Bible reveals what nature does not.

T. What wisdom does it reveal, which nature does not?

C. It reveals a resurrection of mind from the rudimental to a superior condition.

T. Does not nature do the same?

C. Not to minds in the rudimental state.

T. It reveals the resurrection of many things.

C. What?

T. The flower, the reptile, and the insect.

C. But it does not reveal the resurrection of minds.

T. It may do so. It has revealed it to us, and we may reveal it to minds in the body. Is not that nature which gave the Bible?

C. In one sense it is.

T. Is it not in every sense?

C. Philosophically, mind and spirit are one thing; but mind is not the cause of nature without God.

T. Truly. Mind is the natural work of God, and mind has revealed the wisdom of God, as it has been discovered. This revelation is the Bible, which discloses the undiscovered wisdom of God, by minds who have learned it by their investigation of nature, which is God's work.

C. That is true.

T. Thou wilt see, then, that nature is true to God; and when a thing is true to him who made it, it can never be untrue. Even so, is that true to thee which is adapted to thy welfare. But that which is adapted to thy welfare, may not be adapted to the welfare of all minds.

C. Thou makest truth change with the condition of mind, then.

T. Not so. I would say, that conditions change. When the conditions of mind change, that which was true in one relation, may be false in another, because a thing, not changing with the condition of the mind, can not be true to it in all conditions. Thou art satisfied within these walls. To thee, they are necessary and true, being adapted to thy condition of developed wisdom; but thou wilt not say, that such confinement would be true to my happiness, or that my condition would admit of happiness to me therein. When thy wisdom shall be increased, the things which are true to thee now, will give thee no satisfaction, because they will not be adapted to thy condition.

C. Then, what is true to me now, will be false when my wisdom shall be increased.

T. That which is true to thy condition will be eternally true to that condition; but it will not be true to a different condition. Thou wilt remember, that thou must be the judge of all things presented for thy consideration. Laws are eternal; but a knowledge of all the laws of God must be forever finite. What knowledge thou hast of those laws, is true to thee, but greater knowledge will show thee, that what thou regardest as true to thee, will soon not be so regarded; because thy wisdom will see its falsity. And what thy judgment receives as true, is true to thee; and what thy wisdom decides is not true, that thou wilt reject as false. Hence, truth being determined by thy wisdom, must be true to thy wisdom. It can not be true to thee, contrary to thy wisdom; because that which thy mind receives contrary to thy wisdom, is false to thy good, and destructive to thy enjoyment.

C Thou reasonest well; but the Bible is reasonable, and thou shouldst not set up thy reason contrary thereto.

T. The Bible is one thing, and thy views another. The wisdom of thy interpretation is not reasonable to me.

C. What interpretation of the Bible is reasonable?

T. Thou wilt not say, that a mind can impart that which it does not understand.

C. What then?

T. This will show thee, that what minds have not understood, they have attempted to interpret, because what is understood, does not need an interpretation. When a work is so written as to be understood by those who read, it will not need an interpretation, and when it is not so written, it is defective.

C. Then, thou sayest the Bible is defective.

T. I say, that if an interpretation be necessary to understand it, it is defective; and, when minds solicit an interpretation thereof, they admit the defect. If there were no defects, why ask for an interpretation?

C. I want what will make it plain and clear.

T. What will supply some defect, I conclude.

C. That will be a saying what infidels allege.

T. Is it not doing what infidels say, when thou askest an interpretation? They tell thee, that wrongs are in the Bible, and thou wilt not say, that the Bible is right without an interpretation. So, the interpreters of the Bible and infidels are agreed, that the Bible is not right without an interpretation?

C. That is apparently thy conclusion, but it is a new idea to me.

T. The idea will be more than apparent, when thou shalt divest thy mind of thy doubts. Thou hast more skepticism than is consistent with thy good.

C. This is the first time I was ever accused of skepticism.

T. Thy friends have been like thee, and thou wouldst not listen to those unlike thee. When thou wouldst know thy wrongs and errors, thou wilt not expect thy willing companions, whom thou lovest because they flatter thee, and thou payest them for their flattery, will tell thee what will occasion thy displeasure.

C. I want no wrong, nor error.

T. Thou wilt not forsake thy wrongs or errors, until thou art instructed to see them; and thou art not prepared to forsake when wisdom reveals them to thee.

C. I will forsake them when I see them.

T. When may I expect thou wilt see them?

C. I wish to see now.

T. When I show thee, wilt thou forsake?

C. I will.

T. Then listen to the counsel and experience of the deacon. He will aid thee to see what is wrong, in thy mind.

C. I am prepared to hear and judge for myself.

D. Thou wilt now call thy friends together, that they also may hear and judge.

C. I wish no one present at this interview, but the present company.

D. What is good for thee, will be good to those like thee.

C. But I do not wish my friends to know that I am considering a new doctrine. They will rebuke me for my weakness. Thou canst say what thou desirest, and, if I am satisfied, I will call them together.

D. Thy wisdom is wrong.

C. Wherein?

D. In that thou art not willing thy friends should hear what thou permitest thyself. What is good for thee is good for them.

C. What is good for them to hear, I would have them hear, but I wish to know first that what thou desirest me to hear is good; and when I know it, I will not object to the hearing of all.

D. Thou wilt not refuse to hear thyself without knowing what thou mayest hear. Why dost thou do what thou wishest others not to do?

C. It will be unwise for me to permit a doctrine to be inculcated among minds, who are likely to be carried away with new things. They are aided only in the right way by me; I would not have them taught wrong.

D. Thou wilt suffer thyself to be taught right.

C. Yea; and also my friends.

D. Then thou mayest call them together.

C. How am I to know that thy instruction is right?

D. When thou hearest it, thou canst judge, and so can thy friends.

C. But I do not choose to have them hear it, until I can judge.

D. And yet thou art willing to hear for thyself. Why shouldst thou do what thou refusest to thy friends?

C. Because what I hear will not injure them, unless they hear.

D. Then thou hast more confidence in thyself than in thy brethren. Are they not like thee?

C. They are like me, in faith; but I would not trust their judgment, when thy words of honey are offered to them.

D. And yet thou canst trust thy own.

C. Whose should I trust?

D. Whom should thy friends trust? Thou requirest them to trust in thee. Why shouldst thou require them to trust in thee when thou refusest to trust in thy friends? We have not wronged thee, nor will thy friends be wronged by us.

C. Thou mayest wait. I will counsel with the senior of this castle.

When we saw what he wanted, we summonep the circle in the temple by a certain sound of the trumpet. They came. On sounding the trumpet, the hosts of the castle came also. It was a clear, still evening, and when they saw our implements of war, they formed in a circle near the walls, and demanded the object of our mission.

The Commander of the temple replied, "Be not alarmed. What thou hast is thine, and we have no need of what is thy own. We are here not to take away what thou hast, but to give thee more abundantly than thou hast reason to expect. Thou wilt soon see the object of our mission; and, when thou seest, thou wilt not consider us thy enemies, but friends. We see thy arms are defective; and, if thou wouldst fight, the weapons we bring are at thy disposal. Advance and receive, and, when thou receivest, use them as thy wisdom shall direct thee."

Sen. Then thou surrenderest thy command to our power?

Com. We surrender what thou desirest — our weapons of hostility. Come now and receive, that thou mayest know we are not thy enemies.

S. Thou wilt keep thy own. We do not fight with friends.

C. Why shouldst thou fight with enemies?

S. Because they are not friends.

C. Will thy fighting make them friends?

S. It will make them know that they are not our masters.

C. How will it teach them this?

S. Because they will become our servants. Our victory over them will teach them this lesson.

C. It will teach them another lesson also.

S. What lesson?

C. It will teach them, that thy victory may be reversed, and that thou mayest become their servants. What *thou* doest, others may do. Thou wilt see, that thy power may become the power of those whom thou mayest oppress. When wilt thou understand, that thy warfare is wrong to thee, and to those whom thou mayest injure?

S. When our enemies become our friends.

C. Very true. And wouldst thou desire all minds to become thy friends?

S. We would desire peace, but not on dishonorable terms.

C. Thou wilt not say, peace is dishonorable, on any terms.

S. I will say, when minds are asked to surrender their rights as a condition to peace, it is dishonorable.

C. Dishonorable to whom?

S. It is dishonorable to him who surrenders.

C. Is it dishonorable to give?

S. When the gift is demanded, as a condition of peace.

C. When thou askest for rain and sunshine, as a condition of thy prosperity and peace, is it dishonorable for thy Friend, who controlest the seasons, to give thee what thou askest?

S. Nay; because he is not impoverished by his gifts.

C. Thou wilt not say, it is dishonorable for thy friends to offer thee weapons of war, when they have no others?

S. It is not, when we are not thy enemies.

C. Thou wilt say, "when we are thy friends."

S. Yea.

C. How wouldst thou make thy enemies thy friends?

S. By doing, as I would that they should do to me.

C. Wouldst thou be refused, when thou askest what thou desirest?

S. Nay.

C. When thou desirest peace, wouldst thou refuse it, because thy enemy wanted what was thine, as a condition?

S. I would not submit to unreasonable demands.

C. What wouldst thou do?

S. I would refuse the condition.

C. Wouldst thou refuse the condition, if the condition was better for thee and thy friends, than to fight?

S. I would not submit to any unjust demands.

C. Wouldst thou not submit to an unjust demand, rather than to demand what is unjust?

S. I would not demand what is unjust.

C. Dost thou not demand peace, and is not that just?

S. Yea.

C. Then, when thou refusest what thy enemy asks, as a condition of peace, dost thou not refuse peace, and demand war. The condition is what makes peace, and when thou refusest that, thou desirest what is worse. Is it honorable to choose the greatest evil?

S. The greatest evil is not war.

C. What is greater?

S. The evil of injustice.

C. It is even so. But is not war unjust?

S. Not when waged in a righteous cause.

C. What cause is righteous, which is unjust?

S. That which maintains rights. Rights are just, and measures, which will secure and perpetuate those rights, are just.

C. Is war a right?

S. War is not right, when rights are not sought by it.

C. How can rights be sought and obtained by wrongs?

S. War is not wrong, when rights are secured by it.

C. When rights are secured by wrongs, when war secures peace, when nature is concordant with discord, thy rights will disappear. No mind will then have any rights, because rights will be valueless. When war becomes right, and right becomes war, the rights of nature will be disregarded. Confusion will be right, and peace become wrong. Such is the character of thy rights, when judged by the harmonious law of nature. Thou sayest, war is right to secure rights. What right wilt thou secure by war?

S. Those rights which are the inherent property of every mind.

C. And what is the inherent property of every mind?

S. The right to say and to do, as my own conscience approves.

C. Will thy conscience do evil, that good may come?

S. Nay.

C. Is war an evil?

S. It is.

C. Wouldst thou go to war, which thou sayest is an evil, that good may come?

S. It will not be evil, when good comes from it.

C. Wilt thou show us what good can come from evil? Doth war do those engaged in it good?

S. If it secure to them a right, the right is good.

C. The right will not go to war.

S. The right will go to war when it is right.

C. Wilt thou show us, when it is right to do evil, that good may come from it. Wilt thou show us how good can come from evil, or evil from good?

S. The good, which comes from the evil of war, is the maintainance of rights.

C. What rights?

S. The rights which are in controversy.

C. What rights in controversy have ever been secured by war?

S. The rights of freedom.

C. When?

S. The rudimental condition has secured these rights.

C. When?

S. When the American colonies were opposed by the mother country.

C. What rights did those colonies secure by war?

S. The rights of freedom.

C. Those rights were not secured by war.

S. Well, they were the results of war.

C. Nay; but of peace. When peace was ratified, the colonies were no longer engaged in war. Thou seest not that war gave to any mind a right, because it gave different things.

S. But was not that war justifiable?

C. How so?

S. To overcome the oppression of the mother country.

C. Canst thou make one wrong justify another?

S. No; but I see no wrong in that which results in good.

C. Thou hast not shown that wrong ever did, or ever will, result in good.

S. But I will show, that the American colonies would never have been free without it.

C. Thou mayest say, that they are not free with it.

S. How dost thou mean? Are they not free from the mother country?

C. How can a people be free, who are dependent? Are not the States as dependent now as ever on the mother country? Whence cometh her luxuries, which thou seest crossing the Atlantic? Whence comest her language, her customs, her religion, her glory in war, and her manufactured articles which her people import? Are these signs of freedom, or of dependence?

S. But they are free to enact their own laws, and choose their own rulers?

C. They are free to choose as the majority may elect. I would say a majority of such as are not proscribed by law from choosing their own rulers. But thou seest more than one half of those who are ruled by law, who have no choice in the election of their rulers, and very many, who have a secured right to elect, do not exercise it.

S. That is their own fault.

C. Whose fault?

S. The fault of those who are governed.

C. Why is it their fault?

S. Because they should assert their rights.

C. What rights?

S. The rights which others exercise.

C. What rights do others exercise?

S. The rights to elect minds to make laws, and govern them.

C. Thou wilt see who will object to their assertion.

S. I see who will not object.

C. Who?

S. The free and independent.

C. Who are they?

S. Those who dare speak the truth, and act without fear.

C. And who are they?

S. They are not many, I see.

C. Then how are the few to control the many?

S. I would not make war against them.

C. What wouldst thou do?

S. I would instruct them in the great principles of natural justice.

C. Thou hast well said. When thou seest thy enemy come against thee to wrong thee of thy rights, instruct him in the great principles of natural justice, and when thou hast instructed him, he will not trespass against thee. We saw thee afraid of thy rights; but thou knowest that, when we offered thee our weapons, thou didst refuse, because thou hadst no enemy to fight. So, when thy enemies make war on thee, go, and meet them, and say unto them, we are friends, take our weapons; and they will say unto thee, we have no use for them, for we are brethren.

S. The wisdom of my companions agrees with me, that thy doctrine would be well, if all would practice it. But thou seest that such is the ignorance of some minds, that compulsory measures must be resorted to, in order to restrain their acts of injustice.

C. Compulsory measures are dangerous weapons. When a mind is restrained, it is not free; and when it is not free, it hates the oppressor. That which it hates, it seeks an opportunity to overcome, and circumstances may so change as to gratify its wish. The time will come when war will be no more; but it never will come so long as compulsory measures are employed to restrain minds. I have seen war. I have seen the causes of war. I never saw a cause of war equal in wrong to the war. No cause, which has hitherto produced war, has ever been so wretched for minds to bear, as the evils of war. What are a few insults, or wrongs of dishonor, when compared to the wretchedness of whole nations, engaged in mortal combat? Would not the wrongs of injury be abated by the forgiveness of thy Savior? Would he wound to redress his wounds? Why did he not call the legions of heaven to fight with the legions of earth? When thou shalt have full confidence in the righteousness of his conduct, and when thou shalt follow his example, thy honor will not tarnish, though thou forgivest thy enemy even seventy times seven. And when thou shalt do the works of thy Master, the cause of thy Master will be honored in thee.

S. Thy wisdom will not allow sincere minds to call themselves Christians, because they would defend their own rights.

C. Thou hast no right to wrong thy neighbor, even though he may be thy enemy. Thou hast no right to do wrong. War is a wrong. It is an evil, as thou hast said. Thy enemy will not be made thy friend by thy wrong; neither can thy mind be satisfied with the wretchedness of thy wrong. It is not war which bears the name in the rudimental sphere, which we have undertaken to overcome in our visit to this castle. We have not come here to do away with that which does not exist among thy companions, but to instruct them in principles of everlasting peace to thy mind. Thou hast not yet forgotten the wrongs of thy education, and those wrongs have made thee suspicious of thy friends. Thou wouldst now repel words and facts which will be of more value to thee than many rubies. If thou wouldst heed our advice, we would say to thee, and thy companions with thee, come with us, and we will do thee good.

S. Thou mayest stay with us.

C. We have been where thou art, but now we have a more beautiful mansion, where the pure current of life rolls down from the throne of mercy, and all who will, may come and drink of the water of life freely. Thou wilt not return to this castle to tarry, when thou shalt participate in the blessedness we share. We are now ready to receive thy reply.

S. I should be willing to try the experiment, if my companions would go with me.

C. Thy companions will rejoice at the opportunity. I see they are willing and hoping that thy answer will be yea.

S. Thou seest, then, that I will go.

C. Thou hast wisely answered. Thy companions will go where they wish, and thou wilt consult their wish. When thou findest one who will do wrong to obtain a right, pass on; and when thou findest one who will only do right to obtain a right, and who will sacrifice his own for another's good, thou wilt write the name in the Lamb's book of life, which thou wilt take with thee; and the scribe whom we send with thee. When thou returnest, report thy success.

He went with the scribe. On their return, they brought in the book the names of four and twenty elders, and an hundred and forty and four thousand, who came with them, saying, "Blessed is he who hath part in the first resurrection; for lo! these many years have we sought and not found; but now the light shineth, and the darkness comprehendeth it not."

S. I have brought with me a hundred and forty and four thousand, who have resolved to worship no more in this castle, but go with thy companions where thou wouldst lead; albeit, where reigns the principles thou hast taught unto us. Thou wilt see these four and twenty elders, who came to thy hearing, have joined the great congregation, and are ready to live in peace, as thou hast taught.

C. Thou wilt form a circle that I may address them when we reach the arch-way of the temple, whither thou goest, I have a few words to say to them, which will need be required before they enter therein.

S. We will obey thy commands.

The new song was now sung, for the year of Jubilee had come to these emancipated minds. They sang in the spirit, and with the understanding, the words painted in gold colors on my banner. The great congregation then moved straightway for the temple. On nearing the archway, a circle was formed, and the Commander addressed them as follows:

"Friends: Thou wilt suffer no more from the ills to which thou hast been exposed in thy pilgrimage. Thou hast not known thy misfortune, because thou hast verily been unable to compare thy condition with that which thou art now prepared to realize. Thou hast hitherto considered thy own wisdom above the wisdom of thy superiors; but when thou seest what remains for thee, thou wilt know thy condition was wretched, when compared with it. Before thou enterest this temple, each mind will cast his crown into the treasury of reform, and when thou seest the standard enter the arch-way, thou wilt follow in the order of thy conductors, and receive such lessons as thy need may require from thy seniors. Be wise not in thy own conceit, for there are none too wise to unlearn his wrongs, nor too good to neglect improvement, save Him whom we serve. Let no wrong follow this company into these courts, for shame will hide no guilt from the inspection of this circle." The whole company were conducted in order, and received the lessons which appertained to their progress, and which have been recited in another place.

CHAPTER VIII.

FOURTH VISIT TO THE CASTLE.

Mission of Thomas and the elders — The king and guard — The elder addresses the king — Conversation with him — He refuses wisdom — A dialogue with a mind on fear — Calls a great multitude to hear the elder — Address of the elder — Conversation with the circle — Imputed righteousness — A thousand times ten thousand converted, and received into the temple.

After the conclusion of the lesson, the Master said, "Thomas, thou wilt go with the four and twenty elders, and see what remainest in the castle."

The command was obeyed. When we reached the castle, we saw a dense cloud resting over the place, and there was a large number which no mind could count, wondering at the departure of the hundred and forty and four thousand. It was a day of fasting and prayer. The elders aid, "They mourn without success. The Lord hath done great things for us, whereof we are thankful. We will listen to their lamentations."

Presently, a mind descried us, and straightway he went to the citadel. I heard his report to the king, whom he met at the gate. "The four and twenty elders have returned, and have taken their position on the wall, where thou hast ordered thy servant to stand."

K. What is their report?

M. They have just arrived — I heard no report.

K. Then take with thee thy guard, and bring me word what they may say unto thee.

M. They bear no arms.

K. Then go thou with thy company, and hear their report.

The centurion came, and said, "the king desireth a report from thee, and I am the messenger."

The elder of the elders replied, "Tell the king we have found favor with God; for, verily, he dwelleth not in temples made with hands, and we are satisfied with all we have seen and heard."

M. Dost thou wish to return to the fold again?

E. We have come to tarry only while we may do thee and thy fellow servants good, as our Master hath commanded us. Wilt thou say to the king, that the half was not told us before we left the castle. We have tidings of great good for all who obey the truth, and are faithful to the law of harmony and peace. We invite the king and his household to hear our report, which will end thy fasting, and soon change thy sadness into joy.

M. Then I will report thy wish to the king.

I went with him, but the elders remained. The messenger entered by the north gate, and when he approached the palace, the king's servant required us to wait. Soon the king made his appearance, and said, "Bringest thou a report?"

M. I have a message for thee from the elders,

K. Thou mayest say to them, come where I am, that I may see them face to face.

M. Lo! they are waiting thy pleasure.

K. Invite them all to my council chamber.

We all went where he requested.

"I am now ready to hear the report of the elders," said the king.

"May it please thee," said the senior, "we have found favor with God, and grace and peace are multiplied unto us. We have washed in a stream, and thou seest our garments are white as snow. The circle will receive thee, when thou art willing to cast thy crowns into the treasury of good, and learn war no more. Thou wilt not regret the sacrifice, for what thou consecratest to the good of mind, will do thee more honor than all thy works of power. We saw a mystery unfolded to us, which will not do thee good, until thou shalt become acquainted with it also. The mystery of iniquity thou hast understood, from thy reception into the throne of power; but the mystery of godliness thou mayest yet learn. There are minds who can teach thee the mystery of mutual confidence. It will not be taught thee here; for now thou art surrounded with minds distrustful of each other. Thou distrustest them, and they distrust thee. But we have found a circle where no mind distrusts, because they know each other's thoughts. The whole circle need no compulsion to do right, because right is their meat and drink. They delight in right, and wisdom is always with them. They worship God without fear, and love one another without dissimulation. There is a rainbow over their heads, and a cloud of fire by night to warm their hearts with love forever. There no iron rule becomes necessary to enforce obedience; for obedience is loved, and what is loved is not avoided. The Master is not a tyrant, but a father; and, when the father commands, his children delight to obey his commands. What is the wish of the father, is the wish of his children. Hence, no disorder or wrong can enter the circle we have found.

K. Then, thou art satisfied with what thou hast seen and heard?

E. We are satisfied with what we have seen and heard. We will not return with thy permission to tarry here.

K. When wilt thou return to thy new friends?

E. When we can do no good here.

K. Thou wilt not expect to convert me?

E. We expect only thy pleasure. It is not our will to control thee, but to aid thee in the path of true wisdom and happiness.

K. Hast thou not been flattered with new things?

E. We have seen, and do testify, that new things have been discovered to us.

K. When new things have been found, is it not prudent to test them by experience before we trust too implicitly in them?

E. Thou wilt not test them, we apprehend, even as we have done.

K. When thou hast tested them, I will hear thee again.

E. Would it not be better for thee to test them by thy own experience?

K. It would not be better, if I disliked the experience.

E. True; but thou wilt have no experience without a trial of them.

K. I will wait thy tests.

E. We will wait thy pleasure.

When he had concluded, we departed to a mind who was not unwilling to hear, because he had no authority to rule over others. He was wholly depressed in his mind about relieving himself from his fears.

"Thy fears disturb thy quiet," said the elder.

M. My fears not only disturb my quiet, but the quiet of others.

E. Why dost thou fear?

M. How can I help my fears, when every thing makes me fear?

E. Thou mayest be aided, so that thy fears will not control thee.

M. Thy confidence I do not realize.

E. My confidence will be thine, when thy fears are removed.

M. That will not soon be realized.

E. I know thy condition, and thou knowest that as thou art, even so I once was. Dost thou remember me?

M. I have seen thee, but thou dost not wear the same garments? Why didst thou change?

E. I was with thee, when thou didst first enter within these walls. I was thy teacher, when thou wast where thou wouldst not return. I saw thee, when thou wast in a condition that elicited my sympathy. Dost thou wish farther relief?

M. I would not refuse what thy kindness has to bestow.

E. Thy fears will not be removed without instruction. What thou fearest is what should be overcome. I will aid thee to see that thy fears are not true to thee, nor true to thy progress.

M. Thou wilt not say, my sincerity is not true?

E. Thy sincerity is no proof of thy faith.

M. What is well I believe.

E. Thou believest what is not well.

M. What do I believe, which is not well?

E. That which thou fearest is not well.

M. Thou wouldst not banish all fear.

E. He who fearest is not made wise in love; because what is feared is not hoped for, but dreaded as an evil. I would remove all fear, for thou canst not fear and be free. When thou fearest, thou art in bonds, and when thou art in bonds, thy heart is unreconciled to thy condition. It is not satisfactory to thyself. Thy unreconciliation is dissatisfaction with thy condition. Thou wouldst hope for better things, but thy mind hath been instructed in many errors which remain to disturb thee.

M. Thou hast said, in thy pilgrimage with us, that what I believe was true.

E. I said, as I believed; but thou wilt understand that belief is not always correct. Thou canst believe because of my saying; but thou canst not know without investigation and tangible facts. The circle, which bids me labor for thy good, walk not by faith but by wisdom. They are not controlled by opinions or faiths, but by actual experiments. It is not actual experiments and demonstrations of facts which weary thy mind, and paralyze thy industry, but it is thy opinions and doubts. They are the messengers of discontent and trouble. If thou wouldst distrust thy distrust, and doubt thy doubts, thy mind would feel the inspiration of hope. When thy mind hopest for good, thy confidence is superior to thy doubts. Then the despondency of thy condition vanishes.

M. But what have I to hope for?

E. Thou wilt ask, what is there which I may not

hope for? There is no good, which thou mayest not attain. The wisdom of circles, whose glory thou hast not seen, may be thine by receiving it. But thy doubts cause thee to reject thy own good. When the prize is offered thee, thou refusest, because of thy unbelief. Thy doubts distrust and reject the best good. They rob thee by thy own consent. It is, indeed, no wonder to me now, why thou shouldst not advance, and become more happy. I would advise thee, but thy wisdom apprehends mischief from me. Now, I am not of thy circle, thou fearest some evil intention is with me. The worst evil thou canst suffer, is the evil of resisting wisdom.

M. I would not resist what is wise and good, but I would know that it is wise and good before I receive it.

E. How canst thou know what thy wisdom rejects? When thou askest aid, how canst thou be benefited, so long as the aid is rejected? Must not the aid be received to help thee? Wouldst thou require tangible evidence, or demonstrations of its usefulness before thou wouldst accept what thy necessities demand? Thou askest for the proof of a thing, when thou rejectest the only means which can give thee the required satisfaction. As well might the ignorant say, "I will receive instruction when I am satisfied by experience that it will be for my advantage, and not before," as for thee to demand knowledge of a subject before thou receivest the lessons, which will make thee know the truth of the subject.

M. Then, I must receive what thou sayest as truth, and test it by my experience.

E. Thou wilt test it in no other way than by thy experience. All thou knowest to be good or bad, thou knowest by thy experience.

M. May I not know from others' experience?

E. Thou mayest believe, but thou canst not know. To know is to understand by the test of thy experience. The test of experience will not deceive thee. By it thou mayest try the philosophy which we teach. Thy mind will not doubt what it knows; but it will doubt what minds say; because thou hast already found many errors in the sayings of thy friends, but never one in the counsels of thy experience. Experience is true. However bitter it may be from the errors of thy life, yet it is true. Falsehoods even are true, as are facts; but there is this distinction, which experience has established. Falsehoods are wrongs, facts are not. Nevertheless, thou must see that wrongs are true to falsehoods, and falsehood to wrongs. The cause is true to its effect. If the cause be inharmonious with good, the wretchedness must ensue. If the cause be harmonious with mind, the effect can not be wrong. Therefore, falsehood, being a cause, and that cause not being in harmony with the progress and happiness of mind, must beget its true effect when received. That effect is wrong, and wrong because an evil is inflicted. All evil is true to the effect it produces. When a mind is in harmony with error, the error is true to that mind. The error is true to its effect. It is sure to produce its own likeness — to stamp its own image, when received by the mind. No effect, disagreeing with the cause, can ever exist in nature. Consequently, all things are causes of other things, and the cause and effect are true to each other. This is what we may call truth.

M. Then truth is the relation of cause and effect?

E. It is the relation which will disclose a truth to thee. The things, being true to each other, will not be false to each other; so with mind. The things which are in harmony with mind, are true to that mind, and the things which are otherwise, are false. Thou knowest that, when thou hast entertained that which was incongenial with thy mind, it was productive only of evil. It was false to thy peace. It was untrue to thy happiness, because the relation was not true to thy wants. Error is error, only because thy mind is disappointed. Truth is truth when no disappointment occurs. Thou hast sought for peace and happiness in things which bear no relation to thy seeking. Thou hast not learned the philosophy of cause and effect. When thou receivest the sayings of mind, thou hast been sometimes deceived; and thou believest when they tell thee what is for thy good. They, too, will not satisfy thy mind without adapting their instruction to thy understanding. Error has been taught thee, or things have been offered thee which disturb the sympathy of thy mind. They are false to thy wants. Thou seekest happiness. They destroy it. That is false to thee and thy good. Thou shouldst not trust in thorns to produce grapes, nor in thistles to produce figs; but thou shouldst know that nothing is, or ever can be true to thy good, which is, or shall be, incongenial with the sympathy that makes thee a child of God.

M. I see that thy philosophy makes no relation eternal; because, when a thing changes, it disturbs the relation which it has sustained to another thing.

E. The relation is eternal to things which are eternal. But thy errors are not eternal things. I see they will soon be destroyed in thee. When thou hast an affinity, or holdest a relation to things which disturb thee, the connection, thus formed, will be true to itself so long as it remaineth, but when the error is destroyed by the philosophy we teach, the relation is broken, and the effect of that relation must cease. The error will disturb no longer than it remaineth.

M. Is it not even so with the truth?

E. It is.

M. Why may not minds, then, lose the truth, and sink into utter hopelessness and despair?

E. Minds may not lose the truth, when they never have found it. Thou hast not yet found the truth. Thou hast learned some facts. Facts are the wisdom of nature as revealed to mind in parts. The truth is the infinite whole, and is incapable of being divided into parts. Minds sometimes call facts truths; but we teach that truth, which is infinite, so far, and no father, as it has been made known to us. Thou hast been taught the truth in part, and what remainest for thee to learn, is what thou hast no knowledge of. It is ignorance in thee, as it is in us. This truth is the infinite harmony and wisdom of God in the universe. All revelation of that wisdom, is true to thy happiness; because thy mind is not discordant with nature, only as thy ignorance, or education, hath perverted it. Thus, the revelation of wisdom, agreeing with thy happiness, is true to thee, and what is true to thee, as cause and effect, will never be false, because it is governed by an immutable law.

M. Then, thou wouldst teach that truth is eternal and error not.

E. Truth is true to the good of mind eternally, because it is in harmony with the relation of cause and effect. Error is in harmony only with ignorance. Ignorance is the absence of knowledge. It is the mere thing of childhood — the infancy of mind in its eternal progress. But when the infant becomes the philosopher, it puts away childish things. The swaddling clothes of the babe will not truly cover the grown man. They are true to the infant, like the Mosaic covenant of forms to the Jewish people; but they cover not the wants of enlarged sympathy for the great brotherhood of mind. The infant people required protection, and their wants were supplied. They asked only what they received. The minds of this circle have sought for no more than they have found. They have sought to establish their own wisdom, in opposition to the wisdom of a higher circle; and they have found, by experience, the avails of their search.

M. Then minds can find what they seek for?

E. They can find the degree of wisdom which they seek for. They can generally find whatever opinion they prefer, because they will prefer only an opinion agreeing with their measure of wisdom. All which disagree with their degree of reform in wisdom is wrong. Nothing to them is right, but the righteousness in them. They seek for nothing more.

M. How, then, can they progress in wisdom.

E. As others influence them by instruction, as we have sought to do unto thee.

M. Then thou wilt go on; I like thy philosophy.

E. Thou wilt see a philosophy in thy progress which will satisfy thee, that thy errors are of no service to thee.

M. I am now satisfied of that, but what are my errors?

E. Thou wilt not receive all we wish thee to hear alone. When thou wilt call thy friends together, who sympathize with thee, and who have no opposition to wisdom, nor fear of instruction, we will visit thee, and say unto all what thou mayest apply unto thyself.

M. I will call my friends now. They hear my voice, and will respond to my wish.

The multitude assembled, and the elder proceeded to address them. "Thou hast a work to do, my friends. The wisdom of a superior circle hath delegated to me the duty of undoing the errors I have inculcated among the minds of those with whom I have labored. Nothing is more sincerely regretted, than my wrongs. It has been my honest endeavor to do away wrong; but I find many errors, which I have taught, and now it becomes my pleasing duty to correct them. Among those errors, none stand more prominent than the doctrine of imputed righteousness, and the fears and selfishness which it has encouraged. The principle, which imputes to another what he never had, or will possess, is fatal to the idea of impartial justice, and wrong in its effect upon individual responsibility. I have found that wisdom, which discloses the fact, that thy wrongs can not be justly imputed to another. Neither is it just for another to assume thy wrongs without thy practice. Indeed, thy wrongs are thy own, and no one can make them his own without adopting them. When they are adopted by another, that mind is as criminal as he who first practiced them. So, will it be seen, that no mind can claim happiness because another is virtuous. The virtues of the wise must become our own, or they will not promote our enjoyment. Thou knowest I have taught thee to hope for good, because thy Savior was righteous. As well might mind hope for good, because God is good. There never was a time when God was not good, but what availeth his goodness, until it becomes thy own; and to become thy own, it must become thy practice. Because one mind is good, or just, or right, it is not true that all are so. And yet the doctrine I taught thee, encouraged the expectation that, because thy Master was good, he would impute his righteousness unto thee. As well might the claim of thy righteousness be maintained, because another was exalted to a circle of purity. Thou hast no lessons in nature to sustain the doctrine of imputed righteousness. All law, which recognizes equity and justice, repudiates the slander upon the name of Jesus. He transfers no good to thee, which thy condition will not receive as thy own inheritance. Thou shouldst not depend on being saved from thy wrongs, otherwise than by forsaking them. No good can come unto thee in wrong; and so long as thy wrongs remain, the good of thy Master availeth thee nothing. To be saved, thou shouldst not depend on the good of another, but on the good thou mayest attain by seeking wisdom, and forsaking folly. What, therefore, I have taught thee, inconsistent with this sentiment, I would ask thee to abandon; for no good can arise to thee from any source, without thy wisdom shall control thee to make it thy own. And, when it is thy own, it is not another's. Read thy lesson of wrong no more, and forsake the teaching which would flatter thee with hopes of bliss, because another is more holy than thyself. Thy Savior is he who saves. No mind is thy Savior, unless he saves. To save is to make thee wise, and when thou hast become wise, thou wilt put away wrongs and errors. No mind is wise in the wisdom of my circle, who refuses instruction in wisdom, or who neglects to practice its requirements.

I have seen thy ways, and I have watched thy mourning with solicitude. Thou hast waited in hope for the redemption, because another was good. Thou hast waited for another to do what thou shouldst have done thyself. It is this which has wronged thee. Hadst thou felt the necessity for thy own exertions, and depended less on the doctrine of imputed righteousness, as thou hast been taught, I would not now need to correct the wrong I have done. But, when thou hopest for good because another is wise, thou art prone to security in indolence. Thou seest that it is mischievous to encourage indolence, and yet, when thou waitest for another to do thy work, thy indolence is apparent. Be wise, then, and be active to be wise."

The circle said, "Who then can be saved? If we have no righteousness of our own, and are not permitted to hope for it in another, who among us will be saved?"

E. Those with thee who seek and find wisdom, and who will not neglect the good of mind.

C. Then there is no need of a Savior, if we can save ourselves.

E. There is no need of hoping for the righteousness of another to be placed to thy credit; because no such injustice will be manifest to thee. There is need of a teacher to instruct thee in the truth of divine wisdom; and he who instructs saves, when his instruction is received, and as it is received. The ignorance of mind is removed by instruction, and as it is removed, the mind instructed is saved from its ignorance. When a mind errs, it errs not because it naturally prefers the error, but because its ignorance prevented the reception of wisdom. The evils, which mind practices, are not practiced because the mind loves the evil, in preference to good, but because, through ignorance, it misjudged. The ignorant mind is liable to misjudge, but the wise are instructed. Mind must love, and prefer for itself that which is good, or that which it supposes is best adapted to promote its own enjoyment. But very many find their judgments in error. They do wrong to do themselves good. True wisdom, however, reveals the ignorance of their judgment. Good can never come out of evil, nor evil out of good. Temporary advantage may be taken of another's opinion, whereby wrong may ensue to him; and when the mind has received what it has sought and obtained at the expense of another, it is not satisfied, because the wrong never can satisfy what God has made right and good. And the greater the wrong, the greater the dissatisfaction; because right and wrong can never agree, but must from their disagreement war with each other. The mind, therefore, acting wrong, encourages contention in itself, and where there is a conflict, the law of harmony is disturbed, and with it the peace of him whose enjoyment is dependent upon it. He who saves is, therefore, a deliverer from these evils of ignorance.

C. Thou makest every teacher then a Savior.

E. I would teach thee, that every one who saves is a savior. He who teaches wisdom and inculcates principles of righteousness in the minds of others, saves them from their ignorance and folly. Is it not so?

C. It so appears; but why should any mind hope for salvation by the aid of Jesus?

E. The aid which Jesus brings thee, is the aid we bring. Jesus comes not to thee, except through the circles interlinking him to thee.

C. Does he exercise direct control over thy circle?

E. He exercises control over all circles of less wisdom than himself; but we have been taught by others, and they by others, and so on to the circle in which Jesus resides.

The wisdom taught us is the wisdom he would teach, were he our direct instructor; because it would be unwise to undertake to develop mind, only as mind is developed to receive instruction. The circle of wisdom, which instructs us, could not comprehend the degree of Jesus, until wisdom improved them by successive degrees, so that they would be capable of receiving it. Soon will thy wisdom unite with my circle, for I see thou art ready to receive the truth without fear.

C. I have not many fears, but I have some further inquiries, which my mind is not fully settled upon.

E. Proceed.

C. Thou hast taught us, that imputed righteousness was unjust. How can that be unjust, which is freely offered on condition of our acceptance, or bestowed without our wish?

E. The injustice consists in the wrong. All is wrong which is not good. It is not good to deceive thee with wrong. The wrong is not right, and what is not right is unjust. The wrong of deceiving thee, leads thee wrong, and encourages thee to hope for another's wisdom without having the principles and works, which will be found important to thy progress. The imputed righteousness of Jesus will never benefit thee, until that righteousness becomes thy own by practice. No good can come to thee, unless the good be received and adopted. When it is adopted, it is thine, and not before.

C. Thou wouldst not teach, that all evils are unjust.

E. Thou wouldst not reject what is well, when thou understandest it. The well is not evil. The good is not evil. The just is not evil. Evils are not evils absolutely. The worst evil is ignorance. Ignorance will not live forever in any mind — I would say, the ignorance of right and wrong as I understand right and wrong. Therefore, it is not an absolute evil. It is even so with all other evils; they are temporary, not eternal.

C. The evil of wretchedness is worse than ignorance.

E. Wretchedness is the effect of ignorance. The effect can not exceed the cause.

C. Yea; but it may be more lasting.

E. How can the effect of ignorance be more lasting than the cause?

C. When minds do wrong, their wrongs remain, as thou hast said, till they are corrected. Thou sayest that thy mission here is to correct thy wrongs, and yet thou claimest wisdom unknown to thee, when thy wrongs were done.

E. My wrongs were the wrongs of thee, and those with thee. When I taught thee wrong, thy wrongs justified my teaching. Thy sympathies were as mine; but what was my wrong, was not thine, nor thine mine. When I came here, I came to undo my wrongs, which thou hast adopted, and by adoption made them thine. I was wrong as thou art; but what I would do, thou wilt not undo. I would undo what thou canst not do. That thou mayest understand me, I taught thee what thou didst receive and adopt. I taught thee wrong. My wrong was in teaching. Thou didst receive and adopt, and thy wrong was in receiving and adopting, when thou shouldst have weighed my saying in the balance of impartial justice and truth. My mission is to undo my teaching, when I was with thee. Thy duty is to undo what thou hast adopted without weight. I told thee wrong. I now correct that wrong. I was in error. I would now make thee to know it. And when thou seest my folly as I see it, thy wisdom will be increased.

C. Then wisdom consists in seeing our own faults.

E. It consists not only in seeing them, but forsaking them. The wisdom is in forsaking follies.

C. Have we follies that wisdom does not approve?

E. Thy works must show.

C. What works?

E. Thy reform will show thee thy follies.

C. What follies?

E. The folly of depending on others to do what thou shouldst do thyself.

C. What should we do ourselves?

E. Put away all wrong.

C. What wrongs should we put away?

E. The wrong of ignorance.

C. Of what are we ignorant?

E. Of that which thou knowest not.

C. What is that?

E. The wisdom of God.

C. How may we know the wisdom of God?

E. By instruction in righteousness.

C. Who will instruct us?

E. A circle whom we have seen. Wouldst thou be introduced to that circle?

C. Thy circle will not receive such minds as we are.

E. My circle will prepare thy mind, and receive thee when prepared.

C. Why doth thy circle not worship as we do?

E. Because it is not in accordance with our wisdom. Thou wilt worship with new light, when thou seest the wisdom which will be unfolded to thee. Now, thou seest with fear and trembling; but when the pure wisdom shines upon thee from the throne of goodness, the doubts and fears of thy mind will be dissipated with the rising glory of eternal day. The vain imaginings of a misguided mind, will be corrected, and the beautiful harmonies of nature will cóntrol thy mind, and give thee peace, that transcends thy longing soul. The voice of kindness will rekindle thy devotions, and the sweet influence of welcome associates, will touch the soft emotions of gratitude and praise. Thou hast not seen wisdom so pure, goodness so great, hope so unclouded, life so sweet, and society so agreeable, as that to which I propose to introduce thee and thy friends with thee. Thou wilt learn thy lessons of love with pleasure, thy lessons of peace with content, and no lash of fear will urge thee, when thou understandest the joy of the blessed.

C. But why may I not receive the same instruction in this castle?

E. Thou wilt receive thy instruction only where it is to be found. Thou knowest such only can instruct thee as are competent. They can not instruct thee without removing the veil from thy face, so that thou canst see, as well as hear, wisdom in mercy.

C I would not object to leaving the castle, if my associates would accompany me.

E. Thy associates are even waiting for thee to say, "I will go."

C. How dost thou know?

E. I know with a sight you have not obtained.

C. Canst thou tell my intention?

E. I can tell thee, that thy mind is to go.

C. How may I know this, and see as thou dost?

E. By doing as I require thee. When thou shalt see the light of the temple, thy vision will be so increased as to discern the thoughts of mind, and when thou seest the thoughts of mind, thou wilt no longer walk by faith, but by sight. In this consists the wisdom of the circle to which I now belong. They have no doubts or fears, because doubts are the results of blindness. What thou seest, thou canst not doubt or fear, because the truth is not to be feared, but dispels doubts and sorrows.

C. Is there no fact, which ought to be feared?

E. The most fearful thing, which spirits need to avoid, is their neglect of wisdom. Their opposition to improvement is the most dangerous thing which they need fear. It is what they should overcome. Thy fears will vanish with the light of wisdom. They will not mar thy joy, nor disturb thy quiet, when the wisdom of our circle teaches thee the folly of fear. Not every one of thy companions will go with us. I see a mind in yonder palace, who is waiting for my experience to aid him. He will not be aided in that manner. He wishes me to test the realities of my circle for him, but thou canst now see, that my test will not be a test for him. When indolence asketh another to do what belongeth to him who is controlled by it should do, the improvement will be procrastinated until indolence is satisfied. There will be no reform in the hands of indolence, and where there is no reform, there is but little wisdom. I have seen much indolence in this castle. I have seen much indifference to progress, and I am satisfied that no wisdom can improve the condition of minds here, unless that wisdom be received, to give vitality to the works of righteousness. I wait thy response.

C. I will try thy circle.

E. Thou wilt not receive what is given thee without trying it, because the trying is what will introduce thee into it.

C. Then, I can try it here.

E. Not till thou hast received it.

C. But, may I not receive it here, as elsewhere?

E. Thou mayest receive what thou canst here, and practice it; but what thou lackest is sight. Now, thou only believest, because of my saying; but when thou seest, thou wilt know, not because of my saying, but because what thou seest will make thee know the wisdom which I now declare unto thee. Thou wouldst prefer facts for faiths, realities for doubts, and stability for uncertainty.

C. I will go with thee.

E. Who else?

The whole company were of one mind. They all said, "I will go." I recorded their names in the book of life, and found a thousand times ten thousand, who sung a new song on the walls of scorn, and were received into the temple not made with hands, as were the hundred and forty and four thousand. They were made free from the bondage of fear and doubt; and, when they were free, they said, "Glory, glory, to the Lord God Almighty, who art from everlasting to everlasting, Supreme over the works which he hath made; and who suffereth no unclean thing to frustrate the immutable counsel of his wisdom and pleasure." And the voice of the temple was one voice; for joy was increased, when reform was effectual in reclaiming so great a multitude.

CHAPTER IX.

MISSION TO ANOTHER CIRCLE.

Thomas finds two minds wrangling — Enters into conversation with them — Refuses to give his name — Opposes teaching what the teacher does not know — Opposes controversy — Rejects innate depravity — Discards wrong views — Recommends facts for opinions — Explanation of sun and moon, which stood still by the command of Joshua — Nature instructs mind — Wrangling unwise — Wisdom will overcome wrong — Freedom induces righteousness — Masters responsible for the doings of servants — Another mind is converted — The work of the temple harmonious — Duty to avoid discord — The assent is gained — The convert sees a light — William gives him advice, and conducts him to the temple, when he receives a new name, and a white stone.

The master then requested me to take with me no mind, but go to another circle, who were sympathizers with those in the castle. I went where there was a company, who sought for wisdom in works of wrong. They were aided with no light but such as they had found in the rudimental condition. I saw them disputing about something which they did not understand. Though I could see them, yet they could not see me. I heard one mind say to another, who came to instruct him in the wisdom of his circle, that it was better to control by force than by reason.

The circle whom he was instructing, deputed a champion to debate with him; and he replied, "that fear was the only weapon to control and govern minds.'

"It is not the only weapon; but it is one of the most powerful agents which need be used. I have seen some minds so constituted," said he, "that they could be governed without fear, but it is not often their condition."

"The condition of no mind," replied the other, "can be so well governed, as to let them know that what they say and do will be punished with severity, or rewarded with generosity."

The dispute was not wise. The wrangling was wrong. I came near them, and they said, "Who art thou?"

T. I am your friend.

C. So say all who wish to deceive.

T. Did I ever deceive you?

C. Why, then, will you not give your name?

T. My name will not aid you to know me.

C. Why?

T. Because, my name you never knew.

C. Have we never known or heard of you?

T. You may have heard that which I would not acknowledge, because it might be unjust.

C. Then what is your mission? Are you a teacher?

T. I teach what I know.

C. Do you not teach, sometimes, what you do not know.

T. I have done so; but now I do so no more.

C. Then your teaching must be very limited.

T. It is limited; and whose is not?

C. They who teach what they do not know?

C. How can a mind teach what he does not know.

C. As he would that which he does know.

T. How is that?

C. He can tell his views; he can teach his opinions.

T. True; but how can he teach what he does not know?

C. I have said, as he does that which he knows.

T. Then he makes them know what he does not.

C. No; but he makes them believe as he does.

T. Then, when he makes them believe they are taught.

C. Yes, they are taught his belief.

T. They are not wiser, or better, for his teaching, I conclude.

C. They are both wiser and better.

T. How so?

C. Because they are.

T. Is that your only reason?

C. No; they are wiser in regard to opinions and views.

T. In what does their wisdom consist?

C. It consists in being able to overthrow false opinions and views.

T. Is that all?

C. What more can there be?

T. Much more, when they are wise.

C. What?

T. They can be good and just; they can speak the truth, and lie not. They can avoid deception and wrong. They can know something, and be serviceable to other minds by teaching them what they know.

C. But minds know but little, and can soon teach that.

T. Do you know the reason why they know but little?

C. Because but little can be known.

T. No; because but little knowledge has been sought. When mind contents itself with opinions and views, it will make but little effort to gather facts.

C. Then, we will hear your facts.

T. You will hear what may not now be said, when you are prepared for it.

C. Are we are not prepared for facts?

T. I will not relate what you will not receive.

C. Why?

T. Because it will do you no good.

C. How do you know we will not receive it?

T. Because I see your opinions will prevent it.

C. Then what is your mission?

T. To remove your opinions when wrong.

C. Have we wrong opinions?

T. Some are right, and others wrong.

C. Which are wrong?

T. Those which cause you to wrangle.

C. But may we not compare our opinions?

T. What good will the comparison do?

C. It will show which are correct.

T. How will it show that?

C. The strongest will gain the victory.

T. The victory over whom?

C. Over the weak.

T. Well, does a victory over the weak establish what you want?

C. It establishes the fact, that one opinion is stronger than another.

T. How so?

C. Because it overpowers the weakest opinion.

T. Then, when one mind overcomes another, you say he is correct.

C. I know of no better rule.

T. When the rule is secure because it is just, the wisdom of the rule will be established, but the rule is wrong, and, therefore, the result must be wrong. Because one mind triumphs over another, it does not prove the right on the side of the victor.

C. How, then, can opinions be tested?

T. By experience.

C. Experience is on both sides.

T. True; but when the experience is such as to be well, it is not ill. The mind in the wrong will have an unhappy experience, but the mind in the right will be happy. Therefore, my rule is to wrangle not, but let experience test the claims of all opinions. In this way, all errors would soon disappear without disputes.

C. It would be a long time to overcome errors in that way.

T. Will you show how they can be overcome sooner?

C. I think that two minds, holding different opinions, should discuss the difference between them.

T. Will a discussion of differences make them less, or remove a single error?

C. I will say, I see no other way to remove them.

T. The wisest among you see no other way; but have you ever known an error corrected by disputation?

C. I have seen some minds confounded.

T. The answer is true; but have you seen any one correct his errors by controversy?

C. I may say, some minds have been changed by controversy.

T. Have they been changed so as to abandon their errors?

C. The change has been well, because they have received the truth.

T. What truth have they received?

C. They have received the truth of the Bible.

T. What truth of the Bible have they received?

C. They have received the truth of wisdom, which teaches them that a mind in a state of nature can not receive the things of God, because it is prone to evil continually.

T. Is that a truth revealed in the Bible?

C. It is a truth which no reader of the Bible can deny. It is a truth which God has revealed to mind.

T. Will you read the truth to me from that Book?

C. I will show you a passage. It reads, "The fathers have eaten sour grapes, and the children's teeth are set on edge."

T. Does that passage say, that mind in a state of nature can not receive the things of God, or that it is prone to evil continually?

C. It says, that the children were affected by the conduct of the father.

T. What else?

C. Why, if they were so affected, they must partake of the guilt of the father.

T. How so?

C. Because, it makes the children responsible for the conduct of the parent.

T. How does it make the children responsible?

C. By virtue of the law to which they are subject.

T. What virtue is there in any law, which makes one mind responsible for the deeds of another?

C. I see you are an infidel.

T. How can you see what is not a fact?

C. It is a fact that you cavil with God's law.

T. Wherein have I caviled?

C. By denying what is written in the Bible.

T. What have I denied in the Bible?

C. The doctrine of innate depravity.

T. I have not seen that doctrine in the Bible, neither have you.

C. The doctrine is contained in the passage I have quoted.

T. I do not see it.

C. There is no one so blind as he who will not see.

T. Then, I will need sight. Can you impart it?

C. I can not make you see, unless you will try.

T. I will not try to see what is not.

C. Then, you may see what is.

T. Then, you will produce what is, and let what is not alone. I saw you and your companion wrangling about what is not.

C. Then, you must be blind. I see what is well, and, when a minp will not acknowledge the truth, it should be rewarded for its obstinacy.

T. It should not be rewarded for what it rejects, because it is untrue.

C. It should be punished for its obstinacy.

T. It should not be punished for rejecting a wrong.

C. The wickedness of mind must be punished, or God will not be just.

T. How will God punish a mind for rejecting a wrong?

C. He will not punish a mind for rejecting a wrong, but for rejecting the truth.

T. The truth will not justify you. The truth should make you free.

C. I am free; I never was a slave. Why will not the truth justify me?

T. Because it is rejected by you, and error is often encouraged.

C. What have I rejected?

T. You have not rejected some errors, but many facts.

C. What fact have I rejected?

T. The fact that God is just to all.

C. If he had been just to all, we should not have been spared the vengeance of his wrath.

T. How do you know?

C. Because his wrath is withheld on account of his Son.

T. How do you know that his wrath is withheld?

C. Because we do not receive our just deserts.

T. What are our just deserts?

C. The vengeance and wrath of God, forever.

T. How can you tell what you do not know?

C. I can tell what I believe.

T. On what evidence is that belief predicated?

C. On the word of God.

T. Will you read that word?

C. Thou shalt not see me without repentance.

T. Thy memory will not read truly.

C. But that is the meaning of the passage.

T. I will aid you right.

C. Go on.

T. "The gifts and calling of God are without repentance."

C. That is not the passage.

T. Then, I can not find it.

C. But you know the word of God is true.

T. It is true; but not your saying.

C. I see you will not consent to any thing.

T. I will not dissent from a fact.

C. How will you get a fact?

T. By experiment, by demonstration, and by knowing.

C. Would you reject what you do not know?

T. I would receive what I know, and look for the evidence of what I do not know.

C. On what page of revelation would you look?

T. On the first page.

C. That aids but little.

T. Then, I would turn to the second page, and so on, until I found wisdom.

C. Then, the Bible is your wisdom.

T. The Bible contains much wisdom, but nature more.

C. Is nature more wise than revelation?

T. I have said, it is.

C. How can that be, when revelation came from God?

T. Nature is the work of God, and revelation is the work of nature. Nature is the first page of revelation, and the whole which can be revealed. Nature, or the wisdom of God, displayed in his work, is only revealed in part, and, therefore, is less than nature.

C. But when revelation contradicts nature, what will you do?

T. I will say, it can not contradict nature, for nature is true to itself.

C. But the Bible contradicts nature.

T. How, and wherein?

C. The sun and moon stood still for Joshua to slay his enemies.

T. The sun and moon stood where God placed them. They never stood otherwise. But you will find other suns, and other moons, and other stars, than thou seest in heaven.

I hold a banner, and on it you may see a sun and a moon. It stands still at my command, or it moves as I control. So, with the enemies of Joshua. They stood still; and when they stood still, the banner did not move, neither did the sun, or the moon, on their banners. The sun and the moon which were on their banners moved not, till the enemy was no longer able to contend with the victors. I see no contradiction of nature in that passage.

C. I see no contradiction in your interpretation.

T. It is not my interpretation.

C. Whose is it?

T. It is the interpretation of Joshua.

C. From whom did you receive it?

T. I received it from a circle belonging to a sphere, who received it from him.

C. How may I know the truth of what you affirm?

T. By advancement in wisdom.

C. How may I advance in wisdom?

T. By receiving wisdom from superior minds.

C. How may I know who is my superior?

T. By their works. When the work of a mind harmonizes with the law of God in nature, you may know that the doer of that work is your superior.

C. But nature is an incomprehensible volume.

T. It is incomprehensible to those only who do not understand it. It is mysterious to those who have not examined or explored its golden page. It is wise, and what is wise you may learn.

C. Who will aid me?

T. Nature will not leave you without an instructor.

C. That is your opinion, I suppose.

T. It is a fact which I know. I have not come here

to teach you opinions, but facts. I see your mind is overstocked already with opinions, and this is the cause of your wrangling in this circle. Minds do not wrangle with each other about facts, which they know; but all wrangling is about things not understood. I have seen your condition, and know the fact which I affirm.

C. This is narrowing to a small compass the circumference of minds. It gives little scope for thought and energy.

T. The energy of this circle will not be circumscribed by right direction. It will not be without sufficient scope for the wisdom it possesses. But wrangling about things, never increases the wisdom, nor the happiness of those engaged in it. Confine yourselves to what you know, and peace will be multiplied among you. Contention will gather secret remorse. No good thing can come from the evil of strife. The wisdom of brutes scorns what some minds practice. They never quarrel about things of which they know nothing; and surely minds of a higher order need not to dispute about facts which they know. All who wrangle are not wise. All who dispute are not wise. It is a weakness which fools may pursue, but minds of understanding disdain to become weak in the wrongs of wrangling.

C. Then you are for submitting to every indignity, which the weakness and malice of wicked minds may heap upon your reputation.

T. It will be well to submit to that which you can not avoid; but when no unwise conduct on your part exists, the sneer will not be intolerable. You will find that submission to casual insult, is more tolerable and easy to endure, than a contention about it. The severest wrong of the two is wrangling. It is worse than all the insults mind ever endures. Insult injures no one more than he who indulges in it. Indeed, wisdom will not heed an insult. It will not stoop to quarrel with it. It passes on, unmindful of the wrong intended, and leaves the doer to gather what he has sown. But the contention of parties exhibits a weakness on both sides. It has been the folly of nations and individuals to resent insult, and the resentment has always made them more unhappy, than the insult could have done. I was not well satisfied in my rudimental state with the antagonistical elements of conditions around me. I saw war and bloodshed. I saw wrong and weakness. I saw power and tyranny. I saw evils and superstitions, ignorance and wretchedness. Then, I put forth my hand to overcome them, but the torrent swept along, and my hope was destroyed. I was not satisfied with war when in war, with contention when contention came, with strife when mind was striving with mind; and when I came into this sphere, I found a wisdom which gave what contention never brings — a peace that passeth all understanding — a love which filled me with sympathy, and gave energy to my soul for the good of those whose weakness was deserving of a commiseration and care, which the ignorant may scorn, and the foolish envy, but who cannot share the joy it gives to my mind. Thus, was a mind advanced from a condition of wrangling to a condition of peace. When minds wrangle, it is not with words of wisdom, but words of folly.

C. The theory you advocate is well; but it will not do to practice. Minds need something to make them do right.

T. When minds do what something makes them, it is that *something*, and not them, which does it. They are not free, and are, therefore, irresponsible for what is done; as they are only the instruments in the hand of something. Will you tell me how a theory can be well, which it will not do to practice?

C. Your theory looks well; but it would be injurious to any one who will practice it, because he would be compelled to suffer on account of the wickedness of others. Minds need restraint.

T. Minds need wisdom, and, when they get wisdom, they require no restraint to make them do right. They will suffer less from the wickedness of others, when others are free, than they do while they control by fear. It is wicked in mind to do by others as it would not have others do to it.

C. Then, you would unbridle the mind, and give it liberty to do as it pleased.

T. I would unbridle the mind from its ignorance, release it from its chains, and inspire it with righteousness. Then, I would say, "Do as you please."

C. Would it not please to do wrong?

T. It would please to do only right, and, when mind pleases to do right, it will injure no one.

C. How do you know it would please to do right?

T. By experience.

C. Have you no fear of your superiors?

T. My superiors are more just and good than I.

C. Then why do you not fear them?

T. Because they are better than myself.

C. I would not obey without reward.

T. Would you not do as you pleased?

C. I would; but I would not please to obey.

T. Why?

C. Because I would do as I pleased.

T. If you pleased to obey, and did as you pleased, you would obey.

C. But I would not so please to do.

T. Would you do as you would not please to do?

C. I would not.

T. Then, you would obey; because when pleased to do a thing, if you did not do it, you would be displeased and dissatisfied. When wisdom cultivates the mind, it makes it productive of good fruits. They come up, and grow spontaneously. The soil, being wisely prepared, yields the peaceable fruits of righteousness. So, when your mind drinks of the fountain of a higher wisdom, it satisfies the thirst, and gives it strength to bear fruit. It is free from the fears of ignorance and superstition, and needs no lash to extort the required good. It does what it pleases without fear, because it pleases to do right, and not wrong. But the mind driven, is like a slave—a servant that serves only because the eye of his master is upon him, and the lash of his wrath is uplifted to extort an unwilling service. The slave works, but he works as he is worked by the master. So, with those who serve in your condition. It is not you, but your master who works you, that is entitled to the reward. He employs you as a mechanic would his tools; and yet, who would say, the tool should receive a reward for its use?

C. This is a new doctrine. I see you sap the foundation of all fear.

T. I would sap the foundation of all ignorance, because ignorance is the cause of all fear. Remove ignorance, and all fear ceases. It never was a virtue. Minds have operated to make minds fear. They have sought to make them fear what they did not fear themselves. They have represented God, and even spirits, as objects of fear. And they have lashed their superstitious victims into a servitude as degrading as it was destructive, as humiliating as it was ruinous to the welfare of mind. When ignorance is superseded by wisdom, freedom will permit minds to share in the work of their hands; but, so long as mind is in bondage through fear, and works only as it is worked, the reward, whatever it may be, should be given to him who controls. The master, and not the servant, does the work, and does it as he chooses, and by the tools at his command.

C. I would ask, if mind ought not to fear God?

T. How can a mind fear what it loves?

C. It may fear to offend.

T. It will not offend, when right.

C. But, when it is liable to err, it may fear.

T. But it is not liable to err in what it knows, and what is unknown ought not to create fear.

C. Why?

T. Because it is unknown. Most fears are of this description. Minds seldom fear real things.

C. Do not slaves fear their masters?

T. Not their masters, but what their masters may do.

C. Is not the will of the master a reality?

T. The will is well; but the abuse of the will is ill. Slaves fear the abuse of power over them. The abuse will not be feared, when the reality of wisdom corrects it. It will be corrected, when slaves no longer fear their masters; but so long as they fear, they will be servants.

C. Then, servants are to blame for their fears?

T. I blame no mind, it is not my prerogative to condemn. But I may say, when slaves cease to fear, slavery is at an end. The master can not coerce without fear, nor can he make others do his bidding, when they are disinclined. Fear, then, hath its bonds, and those who generate fears contribute to enslave mind.

C. Does not God make mind fear?

T. Never.

C. But minds fear God.

T. Minds fear what their conditions make them. When ignorance overshadows the soul, so that it can only see a twilight view of nature, the mind is subject to the rule of ignorance. That rule will correspond to the light which shines. The whole reflected upon the vision at once, would induce sight to be dazzled by the flood. Hence, in the organization of mind, as an individual, the wisdom of God is manifest, because what is natural, is adapted to its condition, and what is adapted to its condition, is productive of enjoyment. Hence, what is natural is free, not being prohibited by law, and what is free, is not a monopoly. In nature, there is no law which justifies a monopoly of her gifts. All things in her storehouse, belong to a common family; and each member may enjoy what is needful to enjoyment. I have seen a monopoly of what nature has provided for the good of mind. I have seen churches established upon the assumed right of holding the treasures of this and other spheres in their hands, to dispense or withhold as the policy of worldly wisdom wished for its aggrandizement. I have seen minds, in this sphere, overshadowed with the darkness of such idolatry and injustice; and I have seen them bow down in terror, and work in fear before a God, whom heathens would reject for its supposed cruelty. Now, have you not had fears of this description?

C. I must acknowledge that I have.

T. Would you know the cause?

C. You have laid the cause bare in your remarks.

T. How long will you tarry here in this midnight of wrong?

C. Till I can be released.

T. Will you be free?

C. If I can.

T. There is no wrong whence I go. Will you follow me?

C I will try; but I know not where you will lead me.

T. I will lead you where the weary find rest, and the light hath no darkness. But when you reach the door of the temple, I will bid you wait till I gain permission to introduce you.

C. Suppose permission should be denied.

T. Suppositions never enter there.

C. What! no one allowed to suppose a question? That must be a tyranny unknown to me.

T. They will not suppose, because the subject of a supposition is known without it. There is no need of a supposition, when wisdom discloses the fact. All suppositions admit of two sides. They admit of doubt and fear. But where knowledge reigns, where light shines, and wisdom controls, all are of one mind. Hence, my mind is as all the rest, who work with me in the temple. If we were divided, the work would fall, because of its disagreement. And I wish you to understand, that all the work is prepared by one rule, and, therefore, they who work by that rule, must make their works agree. In the circle to which you belong, I find discord and wrangling. It is because the workmen have different rules. One works by one rule, and another by a different rule. When they bring their works together, they disagree. Do you know the reason?

C. I see the reason.

T. Would you avoid the disagreement?

C. I would have my work useful.

T. You see that no work can be useful, which is not practical. The works which disagree, can not be made practical, because of their difference. One opposes the other. Wrangling ensues; wretchedness is promoted; good is despised; the law of harmony is disregarded; and wisdom is set at naught. The whole wrangling is wrong, and he who encourages it by precept or example, is a patron of the wrong.

C. Was not your presence an encouragement to wrangling, when you came to see me?

T. I came to correct, not to support, wrangling.

C. But while you were a witness, did not your presence support it?

T. No: checked it. Had I not succeeded, I should have retired.

C. I will say, no mind should tarry to witness an evil, it has no wisdom to correct. Better leave the evil to consume itself, than throw yourself into the fire to be injured with the flames.

C. But some one must make the sacrifice, or there will be no deliverance.

T. Sacrifices and burnt offerings, which do no good, are inconsistent with justice. There is a time, when mind may aid minds, and there is a time, when it can not. The time to aid is when good can be done, and the time not to aid is when aid will be refused. Let no mind offer aid without good, or withhold it when needed. The need must be realized, or it will be rejected. I have heard minds refuse, because they scorned to be a debtor to any one. They would boast of their independence, when their independence was subservience to educational wrongs. I have heard them decry against slavery, when they were slaves to the most tyrannical of all masters—the ignorance of their conceited ambition to occupy the highest seat in the kingdom of heaven, without the requisite modesty to admit their superiors to an equal condition. I have seen the land of freedom, the home of the free; but I never knew wisdom to rule where disorder and wrong overcame the harmony of goodness and peace.

C. Verily, you make wrangling the worst of all vices.

T. What is greater?

C. The wrong of injustice.

T. The wrong of wrangling is the wrong of injustice. The mind that wrangles, abuses itself, and degrades its associates. The mind is known by the circle it sustains. My mission is to destroy the wrangling; but you know, that many minds love what is disagreeable to others. They love strife. They hate peace. They love happiness, but their folly disappoints them. This is the condition of your circle. They wrangle not about what they know, but concerning what they do not know. And yet I would not wrangle with them, concerning what I know, because it is wrong, and what is wrong can not do good.

C. I will wrangle no more. I see a light advancing. Who comes with the stream of radiant glory beaming on his brow?

T. It is my friend William. He has a message for you. You may answer him when he speaks, and as he speaks.

W. Thy friend will wrangle no more. Let him come with us, and we will do him good. Art thou ready, friend?

C. I am ready.

W. Hast thou realized the wisdom thou hast heard?

C. I have heard what has done me good.

W. Thy work is not done. Cast thou square thy life by the rule I give thee?

C. What is the rule?

W. When thou findest wisdom to aid thee, wilt thou renew thy strength, and soar above the groveling disputes, which thy circle have cherished?

C. I feel no desire to wrangle with mind.

W. Hast thou a desire to obey the wisdom thou hast learned from thy servant, who has instructed thee?

C. I will not disobey what contributes to my enjoyment.

W. That is the law of harmony. No harmony can exist where law is disregarded. The circle into whose presence thou wilt soon be introduced, will aid thee in thy progress to ineffable joy. But no mind can gain admittance there, who will adhere to a wrong, because the wrong weakens the enjoyment of his brethren. Thou mayest now follow us, and wait at the door, till the banner returns; and Thomas, whom we call Contentment, announces thy welcome.

C. I will follow thee whither thou goest.

The morality of the circle was made known unto him, and the master said, "We hail thee as Welcome. Hereafter such will be thy name, except when thou wishest to converse with thy former associates, to reclaim them from their wrongs. Then, thou wilt make thyself known unto them by thy former name. And when thou desirest to go unto them, thou wilt take with thee this white stone, with thy new name written therein, which no man knoweth but thee and thy associates in this circle."

CHAPTER X.

PROGRESS FROM THE FOURTH TO THE SEVENTH CIRCLE.

Receives a visit from a superior mind — Proposition to advance accepted — The seraphim sings — A pearl given — Enters a world of light and song — Description of the works which he saw — The instruction of the Worthy — The song of the free — Address of another mind on the key of wisdom — The seven seals — Address of a third mind — Conduct to the sixth circle — A lecture on social progress — Hope a reality — A lecture on prophecy — Rules of prophecy the same as mathematical — Prediction of communicating with the inhabitants of earth — Predictions, opinions only of those below the sixth circle—A lecture on purity and prophecy—Nature the standard by which to determine right and wrong —Advancement to the seventh circle, or court of Beauty—Sees a white throne and inscriptions—A little child leading a lion—A serpent fastened to a rock—Twenty four pillars of wisdom—Minstrels chant a welcome—Emblems explained - Prediction of events now taking place—Contemplated mission to the rudimental sphere, and how it would be received—The serpent to be destroyed—Evils to be overcome by wisdom.

I WAS next commissioned to visit a work in the advancement of my own mind. There came to us a spirit, who said, "The glory of this tabernacle is dim. Would this society go with me, and see a more excellent glory?"

"We have no fears of progress," said the commander.

S. The progress you have made is well, but I am delegated by a circle you have not seen, to welcome you to a wisdom, which reflects itself upon the dome of your temple.

C. We are ready to be improved. as to improve others.

S. I know your readiness to advance, and, as you have signified your wish, you will walk with me to a scene more magnificent than what adorns this mansion. The whole company within this temple, will form a circle above this temple; and the seraphim will sing a song of redemption. When the song is sung, the circle will say, "Hallelujah, the Lord God, Omnipotent reigneth."

I was in the midst of the circle, when the seraphim struck the soft notes of peace, and my heart melted within me. The melody of the song was indescribably sweet, and the words were distinct and clear. The wisdom of heaven seemed more beautiful, and the day of salvation opened upon my sight. I felt no despondency within me, for the clearness of that mild sky unfolded a glory, that made the former glory appear dark and unwelcome. I was not unwilling to advance with my companions, and no discord was heard. When the seraphim had ended its song, the conductor inquired, "Do all understand the meaning of the words you have heard?"

"I know what is the meaning," said the commander.

S. What is known need not be told, except to those who know it not. I will enjoin it upon you, and your companions, never to communicate to another what is known unto him, lest he be weary with your society. Ask, and you will receive; seek, and you will find; knock, and it shall be opened unto you; so that he who asketh, and he who seeketh, shall not go away empty. The wisdom of the circle, into whose society you will shortly be introduced, giveth to all who asketh, and upbraideth not. Are you willing to do likewise?

C. I am willing.

S. You will, then, receive this pearl. Wear it in your bosom. Let its radiance beam in all your works. Let its lustre shine in your conversation. And let its purity make you free from the taint of wrong. This pearl is of great value. It will save you from darkness. It will chase away the gloom of error. It will protect you from the weakness of doubt and fear. You may let the circle view the pearl, and, when they have examined it, I will proceed with you to the circle where each one will receive, as it seemeth good to the Worthy. He will open a new page in the work of progress. Let all listen to his words, and be faithful to obey the wisdom which he will give you. I am now ready; follow me.

We came to a world of eternal reality. I entered within a sacred repository of wisdom, where I saw minds renowned in history, whose countenances reflected a light which illumined all who came near them. The wide arch of heaven rung with song, and waste places felt the genial influence of virtue. Before us were written in letters of gold the words, "Worthy art thou to receive glory, and honor, and praise, and power." On the right were crowns at the feet of saints, and on the left were gems of silver brightness, linked with a chain of light. These gems were so arranged as to represent in miniature the words, "Poverty and riches embrace wisdom, when one receives what the other gives." Near the entrance of this magnificent theater of wisdom, rose a writing, "Enter thou into the joy of wisdom." Beneath our feet were clouds of vapor, on which the sun shone, giving them a smiling appearance. A vase of flowers stood in the center, and near by it a well, out of whose mouth came a gushing current of the water of life. As we passed the well, the Worthy said, "This is the water that whosoever drinketh thereof shall never thirst, but it shall be in him a fountain of water springing up into everlasting life. Drink freely."

The solemnity of the scene was heightened by the lessons we received from the Worthy and his companions. I heard attentively, and will give as correct a report as the understanding of the reader will be able to appreciate. I will not attempt to narrate all which was set before us, since the simple relation would require a volume of itself; but I propose to give a brief synopsis of the unfoldings of wisdom to our minds.

As we were within the theater of a circle, whose countenances reflected such light, that we were dazzled with the brilliancy thereof, the Worthy said; "This pool, whose water is for the thirsty, cometh from the throne of truth. You have now a portion, which never exhausts or wastes itself within you. It is immortal to satisfy. The current will not dry by using. It is free as air. Nature is not poverty. Her wisdom reaches far above the mind in its soarings. The pool comes up from the well of hope. Out of hope cometh reality. Hope never wrings sorrow from the mind. Zeal can not live without animation. Its worth no mind can fathom. Its everlasting flight is upward, onward, expanding with its expanse, and rising with its strength. The mind without hope, is like a mourner without consolation, like a ship without sail or rudder; and when the water of life satiates the thirst of doubt and despair, joy rides over the storm and the sea, that dashes against the shore of eternity. Eternity hath no shore. The immortal enters eternity when time ends. The mind sees no shore. Days and nights are not. Time is not. The calendar of months and days is no more. All is eternity — eternity is all. Rest is work, and work is rest. The water is your strength, and nature is your fountain. Nature supplies itself, and what nature does, is well done. I need no wisdom she has not, for her wisdom is the wisdom of the Infinite. Deep is the fountain, wide is the stream, and high is the mountain, whence cometh the pure philosophy of wisdom. The wide creation shines with gems of infinite skill. Vast is the immensity of infinity. Stretch thy mind away from star to star, from system to system, from worlds to worlds, and neither shore nor center rises before you. God is there. God is every where, infinite, eternal — the spirit, whose life is the energy, the power of the universe; whose glory the good of the dependent; and whose smile is in the sunshine and the shower, working out the immutable love of his nature to bless the works he has made. The north and the south, the east and the west, above and below, wherever thought extends or not extends, the mercy of God flows like the limpid current of life, and yet you have come here to partake of the stream. I would do likewise; because here you may see its purity, and relish its sweetness. Change has conformed your taste to the water, and light has dispersed your doubts of its purity. Where darkness reigned, fears were indulged; and where fears were indulged, your minds refused the beverage, lest some ill should befall you. Now the fear is gone, the hope is full; and where hope is full, the water will not be rejected. Water is life to the thirsty; doubt is death, because it forbids nature its wants. Pilgrims, your souls have tested the life of water. Experience has tested its adaptation to your wants. Remembrance will save you from the snare of doubts. Hence, the water springeth up in you forever.

"Pilgrims: on your right are crowns at the feet of saints.

Honor cometh not from power. Honor casts authority to rule others at your feet. The crowns of tyrants must fall from their heads, and no mind shall honor the head which wears them. Superiority hath no dwelling place in this circle. Equality reigns, and is acknowledged. No mind is ruler, and no mind is ruled. One law governs all, and that law is love. Two minds can not think unlike, because the thoughts of love must be one in all. The crowns you see, were the crowns we wore in our pilgrimage. We were not all kings, nor minds who wore an external crown; but were all rulers over others. We loved rule, and despised submission. We loved control over minds, and have enjoyed it to our complete satisfaction. I controlled no one by my crown, but by my influence. I saw mind needed control, and, not seeing the control of God, I undertook to do his work. I made laws and executed them as I pleased, intending the good of those whom I controlled. I gave to one a penny, and to another more, as I judged them worthy. They were satisfied with their wages, and did me honor. My crown was not disgraced, as I supposed, because each mind, whom I controlled, received his reward. I was well satisfied with my wisdom. I wanted no more. Others of my companions ruled differently. One ruled by fear, and another by favor. One ruled by threatenings, and another by promises. One ruled by poverty, and another by riches. All had their varied methods of controlling minds but none were more unworthy than those who attempted to control, and succeeded, by alarming the fears of the credulous with tales, revolting to sympathy and degrading to Deity. They controlled with an iron arm the dupes of their miserable deception; but their crowns now lie at their feet.

"Pilgrims: you see a change. You see that ignorance hath its votaries, and, so long as ignorance reigns, kings will rule, and subjects will tremble. Mind must learn wisdom to disarm tyrants. It must see light to escape darkness. It must experience freedom to hate bondage. It must love right to forsake wrong. It must progress in wisdom to loathe ignorance. The change has come, the light has appeared, the day has dawned, the bondage has vanished, and the wrong is forsaken. Experience hath done her work. Mind works for mind, good for good, virtue for virtue, knowledge for knowledge; and equity and justice have trodden crowns under their feet, and hurled the tyrant's scourge away forever.

"You may turn to the left, and there you see a chain of light, linking gems, and words are written. Poverty and riches dwell together in kings' houses. He who rules is rich in power, in the estimation of his subjects. He is rich in goodly things, and his position is envied by the ignorant. He fares sumptuously, and the ruled mourn at their inferiority. Poverty is lean and hungry there. Poverty tarries where wrong remains. Wrong remains, where ignorance rules. Ignorance rules where wisdom is not regarded. Wisdom is not regarded where injustice and force make minds slaves to others' will. Equity and righteousness are shunned and despised, law and harmony are violated; and light reflects the poverty of riches, and the wrongs of poverty. The poor seek, and he who seeketh findeth. The rich seek only to be rich, and their riches are not wisdom, but empty, vain toys that glitter in the eyes of fools, and dazzle only to deceive the unwise. The gems wear not the face of despair. They are gems, inwoven with light. The gems represent minds, and minds form words. Words are true to a mind who writes them. Poverty and riches embrace wisdom, when riches are employed to relieve poverty. They are wise only when used to do good. No wisdom is seen in riches, not controlled by wisdom. Love must see her children redeemed from want, and where there is no want, there is no poverty.

"This circle is the circle of Worthy. It is a brotherhood of righteousness. It has relinquished all authority to rule in the name of God. It acknowledges God alone, as the ruler of the universe. It disclaims all other rulers, and in the light of his countenance we walk, dispensing the light we have received and seen to those who need. Thou art worthy to receive this glory, because thou wilt freely give. Others are not permitted to receive it, because they will not give as they receive. The honor is well bestowed on you.

"Pilgrims: you have now entered into the joy of your Lord, because the blight of wrong, the mildew of neglect, hath no surface on your minds. Rule is surrendered to God. No authority rests in you to withhold when others need. No sorrow will pass unrelieved, and no fear sear the soul, unmitigated. All ignorance demands removal, and he who serves his friend in need, serves God. The circle will now sing the song of the free, when other minds will address you."

The song was sung, but no words can describe its richness. The poor were made rich, and equality pervaded the immense multitude.

When the song was ended, I heard a mind say, "I have the key of wisdom, and I will now unlock the door of knowledge." Proceeding forward, he addressed us as follows: "True greatness is goodness; true wisdom is what will make the mind good. I have seen power in the hands of weakness. I have seen weakness mock at the voice of wisdom, and cast her reproach at its votaries; but the reproach rebounded on her own head. I have seen mind pleading for mercy at the gate of poverty. Alas! mistaken mind sought for bread where it was not, and the heart languished in despair. The voice of nature has been derided, and the weakness of ignorance has assumed dominion. Poverty is wrong, and wrong is poverty. No good thing has poverty to bestow. At its gate, the hungry wait, and wait to be disappointed. I have sought, but not found. I have wondered at my misfortune, and complained of the dealings of God. I have seen no key to unlock the mystery, and my soul has been disquieted within me. But I sought for bread where it was not, and for wisdom in a college of ignorance. Opinions were numerous, and as grainless as husks. Faiths were not wanting in number or variety, but no mind was satisfied therewith. Views of God were conflicting and contradictory, and my mind was worn with the wrangling of unsettled controversy. I sought for peace amid the turbulent waters, but found only agitation and discontent. I was as wild as the sea on which my bark floated, without hope or moorings, save the disputed and unsettled opinions of a dismal theology. In my dreams of the future, social good was never promised. Philanthropy was selfish, and charity not a span long. Goodness dwelt in temples, and virtue signified conformity to others' views. Parsimony was common law, and beggars were common outlaws. Nature smiled then as now, but I saw not the smile. Brotherhood was without children, and conventional limits were drawn over the face of famishing souls. Imagination portrayed calamities, and wrongs sustained the wrong.

"Pilgrims, I have a key. It will unlock the iron door, and show you the secret of all this mischief and wrong. It is a key of knowledge. It is a key which closes the door of hope. It bars the gate of joy. It shuts the portal of salvation. It wrongs the poor of bread. It aggrandizes the indolent from the labor of the industrious. It keeps mind away from its inheritance, and secludes the riches of heirship. I hold the key by which all this wrong and mischief has been done to mind, and I propose to open the door for your personal inspection."

He opened the door, and drew therefrom a book of seven seals. He began to unloose the first seal, when he said:

"Pilgrims: The first seal of this book, represents the first circle. It will show you, that all wisdom cometh to mind by successive degrees of development. The mind in embryo, hath no wisdom; but when nature introduces mind into individualized being, the individual mind breaks the first seal, and wisdom is realized. Nature so orders, by an immutable law, that self-hood shall be sustained, and therefore provides the mind with an innate and natural relish for such things as are adapted to its welfare. It needs no compulsion, or external force, to induce a reception of those things which are congenial to its enjoyment. Whatever nature requires, nature has provided. The innate desire of the mind for sustenance, harmonizes with the supply nature affords. The nourishment is adapted to the condition, and the condition to the nourishment. Self-hood is maintained by innate desire, and innate desire is supplied by maternal condition. The harmony of these conditions is essential to self-hood. The mother supplies the wants of nature in her offspring, never so much as suspecting that they should be disregarded. The child partakes of nature's provision and realizes enjoyment. These conditions of want and supply unfold the harmony of nature, and should not be overlooked in other relations of mind.

"The innate desire is the individual property of the possessor. The supply is the maternal property, and is wanted only to nourish offspring. In this economy of nature, the useless to one, is the useful to the other. And what is not needed by one, is freely given to the other. It is given because the want of the dependent requires it. The want of the dependent is the only reason for the gift. Nature exacts the gift, and self-hood receives the favor. By the favor, mutual affinities become strengthened, and sympathy answers sympathy. The law of God is observed, and nature rewards obedience. The self-hood of the dependent is made subservient to the love of the parent. Both act as nature demands, and no wrong is done. The good of the mother, blesses the child, and the blessing of the child is the blessing of herself, and a disturbance of her love, would be attended with anxiety and pain.

"The second seal represents the second circle. Mind acts with mind. The opening blossom is not the full blown flower. The vase is wet with water. Nourishment is wanted to mature the circle. The industry of other hands is required. The second seal must be unloosed. Progress never stops in nature, though, sometimes, it is obstructed. Mind sympathizes with mind. The sympathy of mind with mind is wise. It saves. Mind without sympathy could not enjoy society. Mind with it, enjoys. Nature has not wronged mind by sympathy. The sympathy of mind with mind corresponds with natural affinities. Mutual attractions never repulse each other. They unite. Chemistry sustains the idea of mutual attractions. Philosophy reveals the mutual tendencies to sympathy of things which possess harmonious properties. The wisdom of the second circle demonstrates the fact, that one mind sympathizes with another. But the mind acts as self-hood prompts. Mind acts as self-hood justifies. Self-hood justifies what is adapted to the enjoyment of self. It condemns what is opposed to its own enjoyment. Thus, its sympathy must be controlled with the wisdom it possesses. Self-hood consults what self-love approves. It is limited. The good of others will, sometimes, be consulted, as when no loss to self is sustained. It wills what will do self good, what will gratify selfish wants. No wisdom above its own wants, shares in its counsels. Others' wrongs are disregarded, because its benevolence is not sufficiently developed to aid the needy. Others' good is neglected, because self-hood has not the love of brotherhood. It is confined. Limit is established to its wisdom and benevolence. It sees what self-hood discloses. Manhood is not unfolded. The third seal is unbroken. It acts within the circle of its wisdom. It is a development of mind, that needs to be developed. It wrangles with others for self. It flatters others for self. It sympathizes with others for self. It yields to others for self. It neglects others for self. It will not receive the wisdom of superiors, because others, with whom it sympathizes, are opposed to new things. It will not aid reform, until reformed.

"The third seal represents the third circle of mind. It will open the soul to a greater wisdom and love. It will do good without fear or favor. It will show what mind should do for mind. It will seek peace and pursue it.

But it is conservative. It neglects, oftentimes, its own good. It neglects, sometimes, the good of others. I will unloose the seal. The same good to others as to self. The same degree of wisdom also. The whole duty of this circle is considered as being embraced in doing by others, as it would have others do by it. The seal of wisdom and benevolence, needs further development. It has been the mission of minds, I am now instructing to aid them. Success has attended your efforts, and reform has been attained. The whole duty of mind is not contained in doing by others as you would have others do unto you. But the wisdom of the third seal goes no further. It was wise to mind, when it was unloosed. It saw a new creation, and the old vanished away. It passed into disrepute. It was respected by those who saw the opening wonder no more. It was a new heaven, and a new earth to mind, emerging from the weakness of the second seal. It was a freedom to mind, which had served two masters, hope and fear. It was wisdom of superior worth to the ignorance of the second seal. But the third seal was not the end of progress. Eternity will have no end. Mind will have no end. Time will have no end. Periods will end. Time is marked by periods. Day and night is a period. Circles are periods indefinite. Years are not known to you, only as the reckoning of the rudimental condition. Night is as day. Circles are as periods of progress. Minds work as circles of wisdom in their degree control. I have aided you where you will now instruct, as you are instructed.

"The fourth seal is now broken. Its condition is good to all. It recognizes no enemies. It never wrangles. It will bless enemies. Your own experience was the criterion of truth. Fear and favor were powerless over you. No wrong was where you labored, but the wrong of less wisdom. It was not wise to make others unhappy, because you deemed unhappiness a recommendation to the favor of God. It was not wise with what wretchedness required, but harmonious with the eternal law of order and love. It sought and relieved mind from the uncongenial elements of social wrong. It was interested in the progress of mind, and the social good of society. It gave beauty for ashes, and the garments of praise for the spirit of weariness. It was wise in good things, and shunned not the truth. It was worthy of elevation to a higher circle, for which cause the circle I am now addressing was advanced.

In the mysteries of the fifth seal, I will now instruct this circle. I will say, no wisdom will govern you from beneath. All rule is tyranny, when wisdom inferior to your own controls. It is usurpation. Nature never justifies the wrong of weakness. It never palliates the wrong of controlling the wise by the weakness of the unwise. Superior wisdom must govern all conditions of mind, to be harmonious with the law of progress. When inferior wisdom controls the superior, there is an obstruction of improvement. Mind is not then free. It is in bondage. The usurper has always reason to fear. The wrong of usurpation can not go unrewarded. The wisdom—principle must triumph. When it triumphs, arbitrary rule will not be endured. Hence, no mind in this circle wears a crown. They are at the feet of saints. A saint can not wear a crown. It would be wrong, and what is wrong is inconsistent with the mind of a saint. In all subordinate circles, there are rulers, and consequently wrongs. Though the fourth seal opened *one* mind, so that what was the mind of one was the mind of all, yet some were tenacious of titles of distinction. They were indulged in them. Though they saw no wrong, yet wrong is not right; and what is not right should be avoided. A title, without signification, is vain, and what is vain is wrong. True, it was but the shadow of things before, but shadows are the mirror of images. The mirror of wrong should not be tolerated. The image is not wise, because it is the image of wrong. Having seen the wrong, we should forsake it. Having proved the wrong, it would be unwise to pursue it.

"The wisdom of crowns, is the wisdom of ignorance. It supposes a superiority by inheritance, and denies it by progress. It plants the sovereignty of a whole nation in the wisdom of hereditary ignorance, and breaks down a commendable aspiration for industry in progress. It wastes treasures upon the indolent, while the poor are robbed to support the unjust burden. It monopolizes industry to satisfy ambition, and wastes the bread of the hungry to gratify revenge. It makes a tool of mind, and then lashes it for its servitude. It riots in authority, and understands not its own weakness. Kings and crowns are inharmonious with wisdom and goodness. It is as selfish to rule, as it is weak to be ruled. The one is tyranny, and the other is slavery. The one usurps what nature never conferred, and the other submits because it is weak. It will not govern without wisdom, when mind reaches this circle. Indeed, you will find that government is natural where all minds acquiesce in benevolence, and wisely act to advance the happiness of all.

"Crowns imply a distinction. No distinction exists here. All are kings and priests unto God. All are well governed, because the love of God, impartial and free as the sunshine, dwells in all, and that governs all. It is self-government, or the government of self by nature's inspiration of love. No discord can enter here. The voice of contention hath its bounds, and selfishness its limits. I have seen the angry howl of war. I have seen the wrongs of strife. I have wondered at the disturbance. But I wonder no more. The love of this circle was not in them. The sympathies of congenial affinities were not in them. The benevolence of smiling nature had not warmed their hearts. The philanthropy of enlarged charity had not united the great brotherhood of mind. There was ignorance of relationship, and ignorance of the wisdom of righteousness. These evils will not disturb mind, subdued by the clear sunlight of truth. Social wisdom is the inheritance of goodness. Crowns crumble in dust, and equity and justice walk over their fragments. Those only are worthy, who make worth the height of their ambition. The hireling is lord of himself, when in the service of himself, and the lord is a slave, when he fears the revulsions of his rule. Poverty is worn by the mind whose work is wrong. It is empty of good. Riches meet the exigency, when divested of selfishness, and disposed of for other's benefit. Poverty is made rich, when the wisdom of reform relieves all want.

"Poverty and riches war with social enjoyment, when uncontrolled by wisdom. This circle is rich. Other circles have need. The links of light, which unite with wisdom, and form that wonderful sentence on the left, will remind this circle of the chain of sympathy which connects the rich with the poor. The gems are minds. All are not equally brilliant. The darkness of wrong will not apologize for neglect. The riches you share, you will freely give; and when the poor receive what you offer, they will embrace wisdom. Poverty is relieved. The poor are supplied. They want no more. The sympathies are gratified. Nature is obeyed. God is honored. Ignorance is overcome. Evils are remedied. Social harmony is restored. The golden chain of love breaks not in twain social joy. The gem of obscurity wants no chafing to be seen and admired. It wants only the covering of wrong to be removed to reveal its worth. The wrong is ignorance. It is the absence of light. In the absence of light, it has wandered in darkness. Neglect has permitted the darkness to linger. When riches are withheld from those who need, poverty reigns. When poverty reigns, the law of sympathy is denied. When sympathy is denied, the war of conflict rages. When the conflict rages, peace is expelled, and with it, the enjoyment of peace.

"You see who wrongs himself. You see who wrongs others. They who withhold what others require. You can not violate the law of nature with impunity. You can not neglect others' good without injury to yourself. You will aid all who need with the riches you possess. You will recognize the chain that links all gems together. You will understand, that the union is immutable. You will feel the shock which another receives. The chain will convey the force to you. The whole brotherhood, from the highest to the lowest, will feel it. The light of this circle reveals but one family. The likeness of God is immortal in each member. The weak have claims upon the strong. The poor have claims upon the rich. They are in debt. They owe all they have to the poor. It is a just claim; and when they have given the poor their dues, all will become rich. It is no robbery which makes all richer. It is poverty which refuses what it does not want.

It is wrong to receive what will make you wretched, or refuse what will make you happy. It is right to receive what will do you good, and wrong to reject it. And you will not forget that the riches you receive, are the riches of others. They are given you to be given to others, who are as you were.

"Enter into the joy of wisdom. Enter into the benevolence of God. Forsake not your brother in the day of need. Bless the enemy in your gates. Turn not a deaf ear to those minds, who writhe in their own scorn. Visit the works of sin, and lead the blind by a way they have not known. Correct those who need with the cord of sympathy, and write the law of the Lord upon their hearts, Do good to those who scorn your message and your mission; and say, "I am thy brother, why persecutest thou me?" So, will you enter into the wisdom of this circle of minds."

Another mind said, "There is a work which must needs be done. The rudimental condition needs improvement. There will come a time when the spirits, as they will call us, can communicate with minds in the body. I see a work of great magnitude, which will be required of us. This work requires a change in the social condition of such minds. As society is now controlled, poverty and riches are unequally distributed. Minds wrangle about the productions of earth. They disown the relation of sympathy, and their professions of love are nearly empty. Sincerity is devoid of active energy. The forms of worship are forms of display. Pride governs the heart. The poor are wronged. The rich wrong themselves. Skill and craft oppress the former, and luxury and extravagance injure the latter. Both are wronged of enjoyment. The oppression of poverty should be corrected. The indolence of riches should be vitalized with love. Society should be reconstructed; industry should be encouraged; love should supplant fear. Works should take the lead of words. Acts should speak for mind. Wrong should not tell her tale of woe. Purity should cleanse the impure. The blind should see the righteousness of God. The harmony of nature should be imitated. Nations are communities. Communities make nations. Social order should be established. War should cease. Honesty should abound. The love, which we feel, should inspire all minds.

"But who will work the necessary change? I see a change in the human condition approaching. I see a mighty revolution in the organization of human society. I see means which can accomplish the result. There is a progress in the rudimental world. The crowns of kings are growing old with mind. Reverence for human authority will not last forever. The relics of other days, are monuments of wrong. The tide of progression will sweep into oblivion the injustice of tyranny. The sun of truth will enlighten the nations of earth. The glory of God shall be revealed, and all flesh shall enjoy it together. But, until the change shall come, no human wisdom can control the disorders of society. Efforts will be made by philanthropic minds, to rectify the evils, but without success. Organized communities will be established, but the evil, in some form, will remain. Something more than a change of external conditions is required. Externals affect internals, but the external should not control the internal. The external is the stream, the internal the fountain. Nature provides that the internal, the fountain, should control the external, the effect. Not until the fountain becomes pure, will the stream be worthy. The wrongs of society, are the manifestations of wisdom in embryo. It is enshrouded in the darkness of other days. The night of superstition is far spent. The morning light of truth must break from this sphere. The fountain of pure water must refresh the desolate earth. The well of sympathy must flow freely, to nourish the plants of immortal progress.

"The first duty of this circle will be to make known the existence of mind, in this sphere, to the doubting of earth. The wisdom of the circle will next be employed to abolish the errors of mind. No sectarian organization will justify the revelation, which this circle will disclose. All will stand amazed at the wonder. When the wonder subsides, the condition of mind will be aided. Spirits will communicate a system of ethics, adapted to the amelioration of human wrong. It will be such as will melt the pure gold and remove the dross of corruption. It will affect the fountain of works. It will inspire the heart. It will correct the mind. It will remove the darkness. It will chase away all fear. It will banish all doubt. It will fill the soul with good things. It will enlarge the sympathy, and strengthen the love of mind. When the fountain becomes changed, its issue will be pure. When the issue becomes pure, the poor will become rich. When the poor become rich, the equality of mind will be recognized. When the equality of mind shall be recognized, the evils of human society will be overcome. Nations will war no more. Brother will signify relation. Justice will be acknowledged. Communities will form nations, and all nations one family. Then sympathy will unite, and keep united the whole, and the whole will strive to promote the good of the whole. Then, the good of the whole will be regarded as the good of one, and the good of one as the good of the whole. Selfishness will be extinguished by the wisdom of universal love and philanthropy.

"The wide world will be the common inheritance of her children. No wrangling about earth, or its gold, will be heard. Industry will be worth, and gold will be as ashes. The love of money will not exist, and the love of wisdom will occupy its place. No fraud will be practiced, for no wrong will be indulged. All motives to evil will be removed, and the mind of one will be the mind of all. Corruption and deception will not be found, for when mind knows the thoughts of mind, the wrongs of corruption and deception will be seen no more. You know that no wrongs can enter here. No voice of unkindness mocks the wail of sorrow, when the love of God fills the mind. The miseries of earth will have no abiding place, when the wisdom of God inspires all minds. The ignorance of the first circle will not be known, when the knowledge of good shall become universal. Passion and folly will not be indulged, when reason and truth control all hearts. But wisdom is developed by progress, and truth by wise counsels. The work of reform will soon commence. The circles of heaven will improve the circles of earth. Wonders and signs will attend your labor. They will be wonders to the ignorant, but not to you. The work will be commenced, when the superstitions and wrongs of religionists shall yield to the voice of philosophy and reason. One generation must pass away, before the time will come. They must pass from the rudimental to this sphere. In that time, venerated superstitions will be much discarded, and human rights will be respected. The work will commence in obscurity, and mind will rise in glory.

Ignorance will scorn the message, and ridicule will be lavished upon the messengers. Time will bring a change. Professions will not monopolize the industry of the poor, nor misers hold the key of plenty. Wealth shall unite with wisdom, and poverty shall smile at the marriage. Christianity shall no longer be a mockery, but its wisdom shall flow like a fountain of water over the world of mind. Dark sayings shall be illuminated, and wayfaring mind shall lift up its voice in praise. The homes of the willing shall become residences of angels, and the disconsolate shall fear no evil. The strong shall aid the weak, and the days of mourning shall be ended.

"I will now conduct this circle into the chamber of hope. There came to me a messenger from the sixth circle. He told me of things which will be no wrong to relate. It was a prediction of future good. You may follow me."

We followed him to the chamber of hope. The messenger then appeared, and said:

"This is the circle of Hope. All who will receive, and do the words of hope, will hear my speech. Before me you see a great wonder. It is the mountain of Hope in the arm of God. On your right, you see the sun; on your left, the moon; over your heads, the stars; beneath your feet, the fifth circle; and behind you, a road. This is the circle of prophecy. Here causes and their effects may be traced through successive generations, and their results clearly demonstrated. You will soon be addressed by a mind of this circle, who will aid you to the desired wisdom. He will relate what events will transpire in the progress of truth and wisdom, in the development of rudimental minds."

A mind soon commenced by saying: "Pilgrims of hope, the mind who hopes will realize. Hope can not be entertained for things which are not. It is the reality which gives birth to hope. The reality is shadowed on the mind with such evidences as conditions will allow. Hope is expectation of good. Mind will sometimes limit hope. It will fix times and seasons for the hope of good, to be realized. The darkness of ignorance suffers temporary disappointment. Hope will prophecy truthfully. Wisdom sees the thing hoped for. The mind intuitively anticipates good. Its nature is full of promise. Its conditions sometimes create doubt and despair; but, unobstructed in its exercise, it hopes forever. We are not without hope. We will say, no mind can exist without hope. It is nature. It is the law of mind immutably established to hope. Mind will hope, and no condition, in any department of the universe, can exclude all hope. It may be dim. The dense darkness of low circles admits only an occasional ray to penetrate the dismal cell of ignorance. The mind of superior circles admits a greater number. This circle sees what other circles hope for. The joy of our minds is the anticipation of good in them. They walk by faith, and we by sight, concerning the good they expect. It is a good which the reality transfers to them through the intervening circles. Each circle conveys a lesser light, until the last receives a feeble ray; so you will see the fulness of hope, as measured to lower circles, actual realities here. You will see the wonder of wisdom revealed in the economy of hope. Minds uncultivated hope in a less degree, than minds of wisdom. The rudimental condition shares in the joy of hope, proportioned to the wisdom of its condition. In one circle, it is but a ray; in another, it grows brighter; in a third, it is glorious; and, in the fourth, it is more glorious. But what these circles hope for, even in the highest exultation of anticipated good, is as much less than the reality, as light is more glorious than darkness; I will say as the sun is more glorious than the stars.

"The sun reflects rays of light. It is the orb of light. Its rays touch the palace of kings and the wigwam of barbarians. It gives light to the rich and the poor, the wise and the unwise, to the free and the slave, to the enlightened and the ignorant, to all nations and all countries, and moons and stars in nature's unmeasured expanse. It gives what will bless, and make happy; unasked, its rays illumine, and banish the darkness of night. The day is not partial. The day is wisdom — a blessing to the world. It is not a special or partial blessing; but it is a blessing in harmony with the law of God. It is a blessing unstinted and measureless. The sun is the work of God. It is his wisdom which made it. It is his love which has ordained the sun to give light to all. It is his power which formed the sun for the good of mind. All things which he has made, are adapted to good. The mind which sees the sun, as a work of God, and the rays blessing all things, may hope for good. He who has made the sun a blessing, may make want satisfied with reality. The sun gives hope. It is without stint in its favors. So, is the wisdom of God manifest in the natural world. He is wise. His works are wise. All things are made in wisdom. Ignorance may mock at blessings, but nature offers no contradiction. Folly may scorn the lesson, but hope expels the scorn. Superstition may have her admirers, but reason fills the soul with confidence. Would mind know God, it should study his works. The dreams of midnight may conflict with the stern realities of nature, but they are dreams without hope. The wild vagaries of uninstructed mind may mislead the weak, but the voice of nature speaks the language of love. Bigotry may frown upon free inquiry, but the smile of wisdom is more congenial to mind than the envy of the miserable. I will see the sun, though doubters may challenge my sight. I will gaze upon its blessings, though bigots may call it sacrilegious. I will admire nature, though crowns crumble, and steeples fall. I will gaze on the works of God, though opinions falter and rites perish. The wide world is my home, though chains and prisons, frowns and fears, mark the circle of those who defy a creed that abolishes neither. The time will come when the chains will be melted, the prisons demolished, the frowns made smiles, and the fears overcome with hope. When the sun, in yonder smiling heavens, is taken as the work of God, and nature is acknowledged to be the standard of righteousness, the hope of the soul will rise above the misty darkness of sensuality and wrong. The sun is emblematical of nature in the profusion of her blessings. Adaptation is seen in the economy of all nature. Mind needs light, and light is not withheld. Light needs mind, otherwise it would be vain. So, with the moon. It imparts what it has received. It gives to bless. It meets the wants of mind. On the right and on the left, above and below, all things are adapted to their respective conditions. The stars reflect the mighty power of God. They shine. They give light. They bless, and curse not. They do good, and not evil. They minister to the wants of mind. They rest not in their love. They are full of good. Wants are strangers there. The wisdom of God will lead you to the full enjoyment of all that hope can embrace; and, in due time, the wonders of other globes will be opened to you, and to me, and to all who will journey to them. This circle will hear the instruction of another mind, and listen attentively to the words of Hope which will inspire you with the promise of good, yet concealed from your vision."

"Pilgrims: in the progress of mind, there is an extension of the vision. Far in the distance, development discloses the reality of things, which mind has hoped for. The seers of other days were aided by this circle. Things were revealed, which have come to pass, and which will take place. The windows of the future were thrown open, and prophets saw the truth. The sight was extended through successive changes to successive results. The intervening links of cause and effect, being omitted in the history, have answered the purpose of superstitious veneration, and worked the circles for whose benefit they were intended into awe and subjection. But the time is approaching when the philosophy of prophecy will be understood, and appreciated. The degree of wisdom, essential to endow mind to clearly perceive the future condition of themselves or others, appertains to this circle.

"The mind who inspires the seer, merely informs him of the fact, which is intended to be effected. It is a fact which must be in harmony with causes, and the causes are surveyed to the result. The seers merely announced the fact. They announced what the mind, who inspired them, impressed them to relate. The mind of this circle is one mind. Hence, the mind who inspires of this circle, inspires the will of all who belong to it. The resolve of one, is the resolve of all. As all resolve, so one inspires. When a work is resolved upon, the whole power of this circle is brought into requisition to do it. The labor is calculated with mathematical exactness. All the obstructions are surveyed, and all the advantages canvassed. When the result has been determined by a wisdom that can not err, the mind may inspire, or impress the reality upon those who have not the sagacity or wisdom to see it otherwise. It is to them, in their condition of ignorance, a subject of hope. In like manner, when the workings of nature are traced in their mysterious windings, and the complex conditions of cause and effect are understood, the results of the same may be determined in wisdom. This determination is also the result of causes, immutable as mathematical demonstrations. Therefore, the seers of old were inspired by the wisdom of a circle, capable of determining results of causes, with the same unerring precision as the mathematician calculates the time and duration of an eclipse, or the appearance and disappearance of a comet. The whole result must be infallibly correct. The science of mathematics is the science of this circle. Euclid has given rules. Nature divulges more. The former are well. The latter are better. The former were true to nature; but the science was not perfectly understood only in degree. The latter comprises the infinite, the former the finite. All development is progress. It is the accumulation of facts in the mind. It is the power of wisdom.

"When the mathematician predicts an eclipse, or any wonderful phenomena in the material world, the prediction does not make the fact, but the fact is discovered by mathematical calculation. All causes and their effects are considered, as well as the uniform and invariable laws of nature. The result is sure. Demonstrations have prepared the mind to calculate the movements of orbs, and the relation which they sustain to each other. In like manner, an extended knowledge permits a mind to calculate the movements of planets, and suns, and stars of other systems. And, when the mind is sufficiently developed, it can calculate the movement of mind. It can survey the influences which control it, and calculate the wisdom which will be required to produce a desirable result, or avoid an impending calamity.

"Minds are stars in this system of nature. They differ in wisdom, power, and glory. The wisdom of the fifth circle is less than the sixth. The sixth seal unveils the future with the exactness of demonstration. It unlocks the mystery of prophecy. It makes hope a wisdom of fact. It discloses the reality of the thing sought. It opens a world of coming events, and saves the mind from all uncertainty. It corrects the wisdom, which makes the natural supernatural. There is nothing above nature but God. He is supreme. Nature is his work, and it is the natural work of his wisdom and power. Mind is the work of God. It is a star amid other stars. It is a sun amid other suns. It is subject to law, as are planets and stars. It is moved by laws. Attraction and repulsion control it. Like and dislike exert an influence. When the condition of mind is understood, and the amount of wisdom is possessed by another mind to calculate the power of attraction and repulsion necessary to produce a result, its position may be defined, and its movements determined for successive generations. The weight of attraction is not the same in all materials, and therefore, allowances must be made for the difference. One mind may be very empty, and consequently light, when compared with another. The force of attraction will accordingly be less. It weighs less than more solid materials. The lower the circle, the less it weighs; because it is empty of wisdom, or contains but a small fraction. Attractive forces may be estimated by the distance between them, and the weight of those forces. When mind is attracted by mind, it is because of the power which one exerts over the other. The influence is proportioned to the weight. The heavier body must control the lighter. The lighter can not govern the heavier. Attraction is with the most weight. That weight is wisdom. Consequently, the wisest attract the less wise; and it never can happen, that the less wise can govern the wise by attraction. Hence, in the philosophy of nature, two bodies unlike each other, repel each other. They separate by natural law, as they unite by natural law. The wisdom of this law is to avoid unlike associations. The minds unlike separate by the law of repulsion, and there must be a violation of the law to keep them together. So, with minds of like affinities. The weight of attraction unites the two, and they can not be disunited without a disturbance of the law which holds them together.

"Hence, you will see the reason why minds in this sphere are attracted to a higher sphere, as we have been attracted to this. The weight of wisdom is far removed from earth. As mind ascends from earth, so attraction grows stronger, and hurries it along with greater rapidity. But minds in the rudimental condition, being far removed from the source of wisdom, are influenced in a less degree than those of higher circles. But, as they are attracted by wisdom, it must be upward. No forces attract downward but gross and impure. The downward force is repulsion. It is not wisdom. Hence, folly and ignorance are attracted by folly and ignorance, and, when thus attracted, the wretchedness of mind is severe. Never will the wisdom of the wise be attracted with the folly of the unwise.

"There will arise a work which will engage the wisdom of this circle. Minds in the rudimental condition, will soon see a light from this sphere. They will hear a voice from heaven. Messengers from this circle will be employed to attract mind upward. They will see who can be influenced by their presence. Affinities, approximating to this circle, will be chosen as instruments of a great reform. Those who will be uninfluenced by the gross works of darkness, will receive the light of superior wisdom. Those who love the world of gold and silver, and are under the control of sensuality and tyranny, will abide the time of visitation, and seek their content in things that perish with the using; but the independent and candid, the honest and true, will rise upward in the resurrection of the just, and become partakers of an inheritance that fadeth not away. When that time comes, and come it will, the reform of the rudimental condition will be renewed with unabating energy; and old systems of wrong and wretchedness will vanish away. All circles in this sphere, capable of developing the rudimental mind, will aid in the work. You will be controlled as wisdom shall direct, and meet the evils of human society with a courage that never falters. Hope will be imparted to the despondent, and confidence to the fearful. All devoid of understanding will revile you, and many will turn a deaf ear to the voice of wisdom. But some will receive the word with gladness, and others with fear. The day will open upon mind the reality of heaven. The day will unlock the mystery of revelation, and give hope to all nations. The miracles of former ages will return, and return to be understood. Human opinions and creeds will melt in the sunshine of truth, and whole nations rise up in progress, and call you blessed. As free as the light of the sun will the wisdom of heaven smile upon mind; and the smile will subdue the wretchedness of ignorance and folly.

"Pilgrims: you have received the promise. Hope, without fear, will grow brighter and brighter, in this circle. You will receive wisdom, day by day, until the seventh seal shall be unloosed. Then, the work of reform will be commenced in wisdom, among the inhabitants of the earth."

When he had concluded his speech, I desired to be informed in regard to the mathematical calculation of future events, and the rules by which such events are determined; when another mind responded: "Mathematical rules are the rules of nature; or, as you will understand, the laws of nature. The laws of nature control all things. Mind and matter, gross and fine, are subject to laws. In harmony with these laws, are cause and effect. When a cause produces an effect, the effect becomes a cause of another effect. Thus, effects are causes, and causes are the effects of other causes. But no effect will be inharmonious with the cause. The likeness of the one will be found in the other. When a cause transfers itself into an effect, or is productive of an effect, it will be as nature has designed, the true likeness of the cause. All variations are the result of combined causes, varying in their effects the modification, in the proportion of the power which each cause respectively exerts. Hence, by tracing one cause in its productions, and other causes in their productions, until the whole are mathematically balanced at any given period, the result will be mathematically demonstrated. There can not be two results at variance, when the law of cause and effect are understood and observed in the calculation. One, and only one conclusion can be obtained by this process of investigation."

T. May not unseen causes disturb the result by their modifications?

"Causes differing essentially, will be repelled, whether seen or unseen. Mind can not be affected by remote affinities. The near affinities must control. Antagonistical elements can not control one another. They repulse; and whatever is repulsive, has no influence to change. The wisdom of the wise must be controlled by the wisdom of the wiser; because folly is repulsive, and only excites disgust and pity. By ascertaining the ratio of their progress, which is governed by an immutable law, and the future development of their minds may be determined at a given period; and what may be determined in regard to one mind, may be in regard to all, when the condition of all is understood. Hence, the aggregate result must be proportionate to the aggregate of the present condition in the ratio of development, as established by an immutable law controlling the development. When the seventh seal is unloosed, a complete and perfect survey of the aggregate condition of mind, having an influence on the rudimental condition, will be open to your inspection. And as all the influence of that seal comes through this circle to reach the rudimental condition, so we know the amount and extent of that influence, and are, therefore, able to make our calculations with the exactness of demonstration. Prophecy is not supernatural, but as natural as the calculation by numbers. It is a well ascertained fact, that numbers are just. Justice is the principle which governs all arithmetical and mathematical rules. This principle can not be invalidated. It is true; and because it is true, there can be no conflicting results. From aggregate conditions, and the ratio of progress made by those conditions, a result is always attainable for any given period."

We were then made acquainted with the principle by which communications from the second to the rudimental sphere might be made. This principle was known in an early period of the world. Prophets and sages, poets and philosophers, have enjoyed, in nearly every century, the advantage of inspiration, although in some ages in so moderate a degree, as to be almost or quite imperceptible to the subject. Inspiration is the influx of spirit impressions. When these impressions could not be made by spirits, in consequence of the positive condition of mind, manifestations have been made. Belshazzar, being positive, could not be impressed by spirits; and the result shows that spirits made an impression of a fact on his mind, by writing on a wall, through the interpretation of a successful medium. Daniel could not have interpreted the writing, had it not been impressed upon him. The impression was so distinctly made upon his mind, that he could not avoid its recital. This established the confidence of the people in the truthfulness of his predictions. They were truthful, not because he was more wise than many others, but because he was impressed by those who were of this sphere.

But when inspiration comes from any mind below the sixth circle, it should be regarded with caution, so far as the prediction of future events is concerned. I will say, it should be regarded as an opinion of the mind who communicates. That opinion may be correct, or incorrect. And this is the reason, why inferior circles sometimes err, and results show their errors. It was not intended as a deception, but as a probable fact. It was opinion only. Spirits of the sixth circle predict facts, and only facts. They do not always inform the lower circles, of all the facts within the chain of events, but what they do predict is true, and the prediction will be strictly verified.

"The circle of prophecy is a circle of purity. The refinement of mind qualifies it to see with less obscurity. The wisdom of the pure will not be disappointed. As all prophecy is the maturity of wisdom in degree, so all purity is the result of this perfection. Mind in its development, passes through successive degrees of refinement, until it is qualified to understand things which, in its infancy, it could not comprehend. The infancy of mind embraces limited views of nature. The darkness of midnight surrounds the circle of its knowledge. A wild and vacant waste of immensity brings no light, because light is obscured by the grossness of perception; I will say, immensity is vacant to the mind in an unrefined condition. It surveys only a small compass of wisdom. The impurity of its condition predisposes it to judge according to the measure of itself. It will not travel beyond its own circuit, and is, therefore, compelled to render a decision compatible with its survey. That survey is incomplete, even within its prescribed limits, because intervening obstacles cast their shadows over the vision. The polar star is distrusted, the magnet is rejected, and the wild sea of wrong rages. All is dark, dreary night; all is wretched, hopeless confusion. Terror, wild and dismal, reigns in the empire of their minds. Nature seems a charnel house of corruption, and the ruler a tyrant without mercy.

"Pilgrims: the cause is apparent to you, but not to them. Viewing the economy of nature through their distorted vision, with their deceptive suspicions to mislead, their ignorance to govern, and their impurities to resist advancement, it does not surprise you to find them actually forming gods after their own likeness, and distributing justice according to their own measure. They can only comprehend their own measure; they can only weigh with their own weights; and, hence, what they measure and what they weigh, must not, and will not, exceed the standard which they have established. All other conditions must yield to their views of right and wrong. The pure and the impure are one or the other, as their wisdom prescribes, and prescribes by such rules as their wrongs have determined.

"Pilgrims: nature has her laws. When those laws are obeyed, the impure will become pure. This is nature; shun evil, and do good. This is law, and this is religion. This is right, and this right is pure in the wisdom of this circle. You will, also, understand, that to the impure all things are impure, which disagree with their rules. Their rules are not your rules. They would control nature; you would be controlled by nature. They would make war upon the laws of God; you would acquiesce in their righteousness. They would control all things; you would be submissive to nature's decrees. They would circumscribe the teachings of nature; you would listen to her voice. They would judge you; but you would not judge them. They would aspire to your joy; but they have not the wisdom to reform that they might attain it. They would dispute the truth, because they have not the understanding to comprehend it. They would reform from their errors, but their rules are bars against reform. They would have peace, but they mock the voice that utters it. They would be happy, but happiness is misunderstood through want of experience. They would be pure, but purity is meaningless in the mouth of folly. They would wrong no one, but wrong is right to them. Such are the conditions of the impure and pure. The wisdom of this circle will acknowledge no law but love, no religion but goodness, no worship but worth, no ruler but God. His praise will be in your song; his wisdom in your devotions; his truth in your minds; and his reward in your works. The union of your hearts will be immortal. No wrong can mar your felicity, no curse awe you into servitude; for you are free, in the dominion of the free, to act, and do, and say, what the laws of your mind require to make yourselves and others blest.

"I will now give you an introduction to a mystery, which will reveal a circle of surpassing loveliness, outvieing all which you have heretofore seen. It is the last seal of circles in this sphere. I will ask, Will you follow me?"

"We will all."

"Then you may rise with me to the court of Beauty."

The whole circle ascended, and were introduced into a mansion resting on twenty-four pillars, which were polished smooth as glass, and over which stood the most wonderful mansion that my eyes had ever beheld. On entering the mansion, I saw a white throne, and in front thereof were written the words, "Purity, Perfection and Bliss." Over the throne, was written, "Nature unfolded by revelation." Under it, the words, "Justice, Liberty, Peace." On the right was a representation of a little child leading a lion, and a wolf nursing a lamb. On the left was a wounded serpent with a spike driven through his head, and clinched in a rock. Beneath our feet were pillars of wisdom, while over our heads the beauty of sweet minstrels appeared, chanting,

> "Welcome, ye pilgrims, with gladness we raise
> The song of the pure, in anthems of praise;
> For wisdom, whose might sustains us in love,
> Calls you, with nature, to join us above."

The minstrels were near a white cloud, and their countenances were expressive of great delight, in the melody of their welcome song. When they had concluded, a great multitude, which no mind could number, were introduced. The first mind that addressed us, said: "The pillars, on which this mansion rests, are not disproportioned, but harmonious and beautiful. There are four and twenty. They are Justice, Honor, Integrity, Fortitude, Generosity, Mercy, Forbearance, Humility, Gratitude, Love, Peace, Order, Harmony, Wisdom, Progress, Truth, Power, Industry, Forgiveness, Holiness, Sobriety, Sincerity, Candor, and Veneration. In these virtues you have no need that I instruct you. They have elevated you, and will sustain you, while I unloose the seventh seal of wisdom, and unfold the beauty contained in this mansion.

"The white throne is not stained with blood. No monarch sits thereon, to rule with steel, the residents of this mansion. No tyrant sways the scepter of rule over us; for Justice will not suffer, though thrones be vacant, and rulers become equals. The white throne has not been soiled by the usurper, nor tarnished by cruelty. It is a throne — a throne of power. It is power in purity, because love in perfection blesses every mind in need. It is white as snow, and the wrong of injustice makes no advance toward it. It is a throne unseen by ignorance, disdained by weakness, and cherished and respected only by the pure in heart. It is a throne of good, and an emblem of the righteous decisions of wise minds.

"Your own minds are white thrones. As you are now pure, you can judge. But no mind will judge you. All judgment is with you. Each mind will judge itself, and not another. The judgment will be pure, because purity resides in you. The judgment will be right, because it is the judgment of self. You will decide upon your own works. No other mind will assume to judge for you. This is your work, and what is your work does not belong to another. Judge no mind but self. The throne is within you. On that white throne determine your works. It is your inalienable prerogative. It belongs to no one else.

"Before the white throne, are Purity, Perfection, and Bliss. They are before your minds. In search of these things, consider that nature is pure, and the perfection and bliss, after which you are seeking, may be found in the adaptation of things to other things. This is the law of mind. It will not attain perfection and bliss, without observing this law. All things must harmonize to insure peace. The ignorant are unhappy, because they do not adapt their conditions and themselves to each other. The surrounding circumstances control them against their happiness. They allow others, and even elect others, to judge them, and ignorantly acquiesce in their decision, however unwise and unnatural may be their judgment.

Those whom they elect to decide the right and wrong for them, are often wholly ignorant of the conditions upon which nature suspends the harmony of cause and effect. They are incompetent to render a righteous judgment, because they do not understand what is right. Erring, in regard to what is right, they enter a judgment in error. The error falls upon those whom they judge. The whole is wrong. No mind can surrender the judgment of itself into the hands of another, without jeopardizing its own happiness. It is this mistaken policy which has robbed humanity of its birth-right. It has assented to a common error, that no mind is capable of determining its own good, without injustice to others: or, if capable, it would be dangerous to the welfare of the majority to allow mind a decision in that which personally concerned itself without the concurrence of others.

"The perfection of this circle will harmonize with bliss. The bliss of one is the bliss of all. The purity of one is the purity of all. The agreement of this circle is the wisdom of all. Each mind will be its own judge, and perform its own work. Each mind will aid each. That which is natural do; and that which is unnatural you will not do. You can not do wrong, because you perceive that all wrong is a contradiction of nature, and injurious to the doer. You can not do wrong, because you are incapacitated to wrong yourselves. You can not do wrong, because wrong is contrary to your judgment. You will do right, because right injures no one. It is the judgment of ignorance which injures another. It is the judgment of weakness which inflicts wrong for wrong, and renders evil for evil. None but oppressors will be cruel, vindictive, or unjust. Oppression is the power of folly. It is the work of tyrants. It is the wrong of ignorance. Governments are impure. They compel the ignorant to do wrong. They violate the laws of nature. They impose burdens on the poor, and grant favors to the rich. They levy contributions on property to give honor to the indolent. They make laws for the people to restrain the enjoyment of mind; and they punish crimes, which their laws have made, without mercy. They refuse instruction from heaven, because heaven is not a monopoly adapted to their selfish wisdom.

"They bow before a throne — a throne black as midnight. They bow in darkness, and receive the lash of oppression. They bow in smiles, and rise in tears. There is a tyrant on the throne. He judges evil good, and good evil. He is judge; and he judges after his own heart. Alas! the throne is impure. The pool of wisdom has not been polluted with his infirmities. Nature will wash away the wrongs of ignorance. Experience will remove the cruelty of darkness. Progress will unveil the miseries of deception. Favoritism will not rob pauperism. Folly will not eclipse wisdom. Fear will not paralyze industry, and wrong will not rule over right. Then, purity will not center in profession without goodness, nor perfection be a dead language in the throne of judgment.

"Pilgrims: all bliss is the exercise of goodness. Love is the divinity of the universe. Hate is the hell of fools. Affection is the element of heaven. Sympathy is the law of nature. Ignorance is the mother of crime. Crime is the father of misery. Misery is hell — bliss is heaven. Show yourselves pure, and heaven is within you. Show yourselves good, and bliss will not forsake you. Show yourselves wise, and purity will develop itself; and, when purity develops itself, no evil can befall you. The righteous shall fear no evil. The pure shall see good. The bliss of wisdom shall grow brighter and brighter, forever.

"Pilgrims: you will be required to develop great mysteries to the rudimental world. Nature must be unfolded to the ignorant. The undeveloped mind must be expanded. The angry waters of contention must be stilled. The wild sea of disturbance must be calmed. The midnight of deception must pass away. The clear sunlight of nature must open the treasures of your path. You will transmit the realities of this sphere to earth's inhabitants. The mighty must overcome the weakness of infancy. The strong must raise up the sorrowing, the despondent, and the wretched. The wise must instruct the unwise; and upon you will devolve the work of correcting the wrongs and errors of humanity. The former days will return, when, through your instrumentality, the wilderness of uncultivated mind shall arise in the strength of wisdom, and nature smile with the song of redemption. You must go to the boasted land of the free, and publish the tidings of immortality. You will not sound an alarm of danger, but you will write the law of love in the hearts of the children of men. You will inspire minds with hope, and expel the darkness of the grave. You will turn many from paths of folly, and put the wisdom of nature in their souls. You will reform many, and the many will reform more, until the nations of the earth shall seek peace, and bliss find a residence in the temple of God. You will meet no opposition you will not overcome, nor will you tire in your labor, until the poor shall be made rich, and the wants of humanity shall become satisfied with the luxury of true blessedness.

"There is a light which you will emit in your pathway,

that will cause pure minds to rejoice, and the impure to tremble with fear. Preparatory to the dawning of that day upon the world below, it will be your work to get your means in readiness, so as to effectually accomplish the pleasure of God, in the removal of wrong. You will need wisdom, adapted to the conditions of those whom you will instruct, and adequate to the great ends of human development. You will have means. The means which nature affords are equal to every want. There never can be a famine, when every want is supplied. The white throne of judgment will admit no error. It is the throne of God, of nature, and of your own hearts. It is within, around, above, and below you. From this throne you will dispense justice to the needy, liberty to the captive, and peace to the world. You will go where need calls you, and where you can do good. You will not waste your strength in vain. You will operate with great power, when circumstances make it expedient. You will show signs of your presence, and the wisdom of the world will be humbled. Philosophers will be confounded, and ignorance will mock, but can not resist. You will teach the little child how to control the lion that growls at the disclosure. You will lead the strong man by an influence which he will not acknowledge. He will not yield until the child commands. The world of mind will not yield to the voice of nature, until nature reveals her philosophy. That world of mind is in its boasted strength a lion, but the little child, the weak things, as they will call your manifestations, will control the lion. Nature will arm the weak with wisdom, to control a great multitude. They will be strong, and the lion will feel his weakness. He will roar no more when the child touches his heart. He will not harm, nor be harmed, when no want induces him to seek for blood. The day will come, when the wants of the lion will be satisfied without wrong. The day will come, when the wants of mind will be satisfied with good things. The day will come, when you will converse with the rudimental world, as you do with each other. The day will come, when the wisdom of the two spheres will meet. In that day you will rejoice, because great good will be done. In that day, the invisible things of God will be clearly seen, being manifest by the things which are made. They will be manifest through you, and minds will be inspired to write the things which they have seen. The works of nature will not retrograde; the progress of truth will onward move, till one family, and no more, shall inhabit the earth. That family shall be one, and all nations shall unite in it. The common ties of sympathy and justice shall be felt, and neglect shall be no more known, for all mind will be inspired with your love and peace.

"The representation of a serpent fastened in the rock, will show you, that the subtlety and low sensuality of mind will be powerless against your efforts. The serpent will not injure you, nor retard by his energy the work committed to your hands. Indeed, you know that none but such as hug the earth, as this serpent represents, can oppose the wisdom you will disclose. They only who covet, like creeping things, the earth, and who drag their bodies in a serpentine course along the road of human life, will not look up to heaven for support and wisdom; but you will not be overcome by their will; for their ignorance is not unconquerable. You will receive, in due time, all the instructions which will be necessary, and enter upon your mission with alacrity. But you may ask, what may we do to get things in readiness? You will now be instructed by another mind."

When he had concluded, another mind said:

"Pilgrims: the means requisite to success, in your mission to the rudimental sphere, are few and simple. You will need wisdom and prudence. You will require patience and perseverance. With these qualities, you will prosper in the work allotted you. In the first place, you will be wise to select such mediums as will do good, and not conceal the facts which shall be made manifest. You will select such as will be faithful in the work of revealing the truth. You will select such as you can find who will not turn aside from the manifestations you will make, because popular scorn shall be hissed at the philosophy you may teach. You will select such as will not crawl serpent-like to gratify the low aspirations of a defunct religion, or a brutal, deceptive, sensuality, which will envy what it has not the industry or ambition to investigate, and reduce to practice. Take such as you can find, who will not bow to the dust, because weakness is not able to stand erect, and face the evils of misguided mind. Take such as will not disown heaven to gratify lust and earth. Take such as will not wrong your message by concealing it under a bushel. Take such as will do the work of revealment.

"The mission will be commenced in about twenty-five years. It will be opposed with great violence by religionists. The superstitious will charge your work to evil spirits, and the skeptical will not. The condition of mind in the rudimental world, will require a great many manifestations to improve it. There will arise minds who will not believe the evidence of their own senses. They will be moved, and see things moved; and, when they see and know the facts, they will seek to find some cause other than spirits, which they will imagine have produced it. They will be moved, and say that they moved themselves. They will be instructed, and say that instruction is of themselves. They will contrive every possible means to gainsay the facts. They will attribute the manifestations to a cause, which is not, and never can be, the real one. They will say, mind is conscious and unconscious. They will contradict themselves. No mind can be conscious and unconscious. No mind can be moved, and move itself. No mind can do what you will do, and not be conscious that it did it. You will write what will be known and unknown to others. They will say, they thought it, because you impressed the thought. They will say, they moved themselves, because you moved them. They will write what you impress, and as you move them; but they will say, it was their impressions and not yours. They will write what is not impressed or known to them, and they will impute the writing to others in the body. They will write without impressions, and they will say, it is electricity. They will turn all evidence into imagination, and then demand greater evidence from you.

"Such will be the condition of mind. Others will receive the evidence and progress in wisdom. You will give to every mind all within your power; but you will bear this message to mind: That what may gratify idle curiosity, is the work of idlers; but what is necessary to develop mind, is a candid investigation of the laws by which it is governed. The wise will reform, but the unwise will cavil, because they can not control you. You will write what will do good, and when your message shall be discarded, or your mission disputed, you will go to such as will hear you, and be benefited by your efforts to do good.

"I shall now instruct you in regard to the serpent. I shall give you, spike and a sledge. You will drive the spike through the head of the serpent, and clinch it in a rock. The serpent is the adversary of reform. It is the deceiver of mind. Its path is secluded and vile. It loathes progress. It wishes the old den for its habitation. It lurks among rocks, and secludes itself in crevices. It wants nothing new, and bites to destroy. The spike is truth. Take it; use it; for that which is evil, it is good to control. The evil is in mind. The serpent lives only where evil reigns. Where evil reigns fix your weapon. The evil is opposition to holiness; it is opposition to good; and when you fix your weapon of truth in the head of error and wrong, let the mighty power of wisdom drive the spike through the head of the serpent, that it may die a death without mourning.

"The serpent is an emblem of earthly folly. It is deceptive and vile. It shuns the path of the wise and good. It crawls noiselessly into the mind. It bites the good of the soul. It induces despair and shame. It wins minds from rectitude and confidence. It is not mind, but the deceiver of mind. Its deceptions are practiced, where its influence prevails. Its influence prevails where evils exist. It is evil. It is nothing but evil. You will wrong no one by destroying it. To destroy evil, you will use the wisdom of this circle. You will overcome the evils of ignorance. But ignorance will war against the truth. All the machinery of war will be brought against it. The work will commence in a day of darkness, and the morning light will dissipate the gloom of doubt. The sadness of despair will vanish before the joy of eternal wisdom.

"The rudimental world is afflicted with great evils.

These evils are in all the conditions of human society. They enter into the composition of all human governments, the religious institutions, all classes of mind; and science and philosophy, as understood, have not the power to correct them. Science and philosophy are corrupted with the errors and wrongs of ignorance. The wisdom of this circle must displace those wrongs. It must eradicate the woes, and harmonize the antagonisms of mind. The old forms of government must give place to new. The new must give order and beauty, purity and justice to universal mind. It must correct the unhealthy current of wrong. It must vitalize the soul of humanity with good. It must remove the poison of the serpent from the hearts of men. It must satisfy the wants of nature with nature's blessings. It must overcome the wrongs of society with the rights of mankind. These rights must be asserted and proclaimed, until they shall be understood and appreciated, obeyed and adopted, as the rule of happiness.

"Then, the dishonesty of mind will not hypocritically reverence what it practically denies. Then, the votaries of creeds will not blush to be the friends of truth, nor covet the wrongs of oppression to correct the natural convictions of free inquiry. You will work a reform of long-standing abuses. The stipendiaries of religious munificence will not oppose the voice which gives freedom, and the old theories of exclusive prerogatives, which subvert the equitable rights of universal humanity, will be venerated no more. There must be a great change in the social condition to remove the social evils of mind. You will remove the barriers of progress, by removing the fears which repel investigation. The wrong of fear must be overcome. The slave of tyrannical rule must be set free from his chains. The mind must be taught to respect its own rights, and disown the usurper's pretensions. It must be taught that wisdom is not tyranny, and that nature will not justify submission. It must be taught the nature of its own powers, and be inspired to respect its own competency to rule itself, without the interposition of arbitrary force."

Such is a brief synopsis of the instruction, appertaining to our ingress into the seventh circle. I shall, hereafter, allude to some other things, which I do not, at present see fit to disclose. When the lectures were concluded, I was impressed with the importance of commencing the work of reform among the circles of earth. It was not my project exclusively, but the whole circle. We sought to make manifestations in various places. I accompanied a great number of minds to different localities, but saw the force of opposition, and the predisposition of the minds in the rudimental sphere, to be so tenaciously inclined to superstition and veneration of ancient theologies, that we determined, in the first place, to overcome the impediments in our path, by removing the superstition and relaxing the confidence of mind in the multiplicity of opinions and dogmas, which were being promulgated. Accordingly, we sought to prepare minds for the influx of communications by special impressions of facts upon them. The impressions have been verified, and the verification has induced wonder on the part of the impressed. In many instances, future events have been so impressed by spirits on the minds of susceptible persons, as to leave no doubt of the reality. These impressions obtained the name of presentiments. They were presentiments, and the presentiments of those who dwelt in the second sphere. Impressions of facts have been regarded also, as fore-warnings;

and, in some instances, they were, but not always. The mind has conjectured many things as the cause, without suspecting the true one. It has felt afraid of acknowledging, that some guardian spirit has produced these impressions, as though it would be a dishonor to them, or that the thought would be impious and ridiculous. Under these circumstances, we gradually affected mind, until it was clearly seen, that public opinion would not justify martyrdom; when the work of reforming minds from the abuses to which they had long been exposed, was, commenced with a view to relieve it. That work is now in progress. It is begun.

CHAPTER XI.

MISSION TO THE RUDIMENTAL SPHERE.

Franklin, Swedenborg, Paine, and his companions visit a place near the castle — Old things become new — Process of change — Identity preserved — Self is a part of the body — All sympathize together in good and ill — Governments defective — Opposition to capital punishment — Origin of evil — How overcome — Success of the mission — Means must be adapted to conditions — Contradictory communications develop the condition of minds in the second sphere — Conflicting revealments harmonious with different degrees of wisdom —Writing mediums—Societies and forms of worship —Adaptation is harmony —Harmony should not be disturbed —The mission of spirits will be to regulate minds —Minds will change forms —Retire to a mansion —Onward is a passport —Dullness reproved —Dedication of the Pilgrimage.

When the instructions were given, I said to my companion, "You will now request William to make a journey with us."

"Shall we not be aided with others?" said she.

"Others will come with us," I replied.

Presently Benjamin Franklin and Emanuel Swedenborg, as they were called in the rudimental sphere, went with us to a place near the old castle, but which was more elevated in wisdom, and less incredulous of progress. On approaching it, William said: "Thou seest nothing new in this place."

T. I see new things have become old.

W. Thou wilt see old things become new. Behold, we make all things new.

T. Thou canst not make a new creation.

W. We can create new things out of old.

T. We can change old things into new.

W. Thou wilt change nothing new into old.

The mind of one with whom I had formed an acquaintance in the body, responded: "How will you change old things into new?"

W. Thou seest a change in nature. Thou seest not the change which nature produces, until it is produced. The wisdom of God in nature works great changes. The blossom is not as the fruit, nor the seed as the blossom. The voice which nature utters, is a voice thou wilt not deny. It is the voice of God to thee. Dost thou hear it, and dost thou feel it? The young ravens cry, and their cry is heard. The wail of want finds a response in the supply which sympathy affords. That sympathy is natural; and, in its exercise, the unfledged wing becomes invigorated, and change gives support to the dependent. So, in thy weakness, thou hast received aid from sympathy, until change gave thee strength to aid others. Sympathy is the divinity of nature. It controls even animals. It will control enemies. It is a divinity that no enemy can resist. It will conquer. It will change the old into new. The barren field will become the fruitful vineyard. The dormant energies will be quickened. The inactive powers will become active, and change will make all things new.

M. If all things become changed by progress, will not all things lose their original identity?

W. The change is not external, but is internal. The change is pure. The grossness of impurity, being removed, allows a work of refinement to take place, so that the divinity of sympathy may be exercised without obstruction. In its progress, the refinement will expand the charity of the soul, and divest it of all wrong. When it is divested of all wrong, it will feel inspired with benevolence. This benevolence will become extended, until all nature smiles with the love of God, and all minds are linked together forming a chain of affinity co-extensive with the whole world, in heaven and on earth, and united by an immortal tie which no change will dissolve, but strengthen, forever and ever.

On arriving at the designated place, there were many minds conversing about the motives of works. One said, that no motive could be pure, unless a mind realized some good to itself; another said, all good of self should be overlooked; and a third said, no mind could overlook the good of itself. We heard the conversation, when William asked, "How can self be overlooked, when self is a part of the body, of which all are members?"

"Ought not selfishness to be overcome, so that others' good may be advanced?" said a mind.

W. Thou wilt understand, that no mind can be disinterested in its welfare, however much it may desire to overcome the nature which is selfish, and consults selfish good. The good of self is well, and what is well should not be overcome. It is necessary to the good of all. Self is a part of all. If a part be not well, the whole can not be, as the whole is made up of parts. When one part is neglected, the other parts will suffer. Thy mind is a part of the great body of mind. It is dependent on the body, and the body is dependent on it. These parts embrace the whole family of mankind. There can be no joy without all the parts participate in it, neither can there be sorrow, without all sympathize in it. Thou wilt see that minds are united by the law of sympathy in one body. The sympathy is natural, and when one part monopolizes the control of the other to its disadvantage, it must sympathetically suffer for its folly. It will not be happy in any disturbance of the rest.

M. Then, are not minds disturbing their own happiness, when they neglect those with whom they are united?

W. Thou wilt see that governments and societies, in the rudimental world, deny the law of God, which should govern all his works. They unite in compacts for the purpose of promoting the public good; but the compacts do not seem to understand that sympathy is not a law which grants favors to one and withholds them from another. In all human governments, you will find that the few who control, make slaves of the many who are controlled. The ruler should fare as the ruled, and know that injuries inflicted upon the latter, will result in his injury. There should be no favoritism of one part over another. Governments study to govern; and, in order to govern, coercive measures are adopted. The governed must submit, and pay the expense of their own folly. They must not disobey their rulers, because their rulers will enforce either the law or their own authority, to induce submission. No matter what the cost may be; it must be borne by the ruled. When the ruled consent to be ruled, they should not refuse the cost; but when rulers ask submission to rules which are obnoxious to the good of one part for the support of another part, they are wanting in wisdom, and their demands will be rejected, when the ruled understand their own wants, and the means which are essential to their gratification. The wisdom of the ruler consults his own supposed good. He wants what will make him respected and happy. But, being aided only by a narrow and limited wisdom, he sees not the wisdom of nature's laws. He sees not the dependence of one part upon the other; and, consequently, he rules in wisdom of self, or in the wisdom of ignorance of the relation on which enjoyment depends. Now, he should love self, and he should neglect no means which are necessary to produce his own happiness; but, when he rules over others, he should understand that, if he injure them, he injures himself; or, if he benefit them, he does good to himself. An injury done to one person by a ruler, is an injury to all. Hence, no government is as pure as it should be, which wrongs one to govern the many. I have seen men, educated in crime by law ordained, condemned and wronged by law. I have seen a mind who had been taught the law of death for death, wronged by the instruction. It was a mind who once resided in Philadelphia. I knew the mind when he was in his childhood. I have often wondered, that my adopted commonwealth should have engrafted upon their criminal code, so barbarous and cruel a law as the death penalty. I saw that young man in his childhood taught the doctrine of revenge. I heard his parents justify death for death, and express even gratification, when some poor criminal had expiated the death penalty. The child imbibed the horrid teaching. The parents verily believed the lesson salutary upon their son. But the son felt the malice, the wrong, the wrangling in his mind, struggling against sympathy, until sympathy yielded to the wrong. I saw him again. The gallows was his death bed. The parents had taken the farewell interview. The executioner inquired of the criminal, if he wished to say any thing to the spectators. The young man made a brief speech. He said: "The sentence of the law is about to be executed upon me. I have sinned against God, but I hope for mercy in Christ. I have no ill will to any one. I acknowledge that my sentence is just. I hope this may be a warning to all, not to do as I have done. May God have mercy on my soul." He was killed. The people said, "It was just." But when the mind reached this sphere, it was corrected. It was disabused of its malignity. It was educated in the knowledge of nature. It was disrobed of its cruel garments. It was taught the divinity of natural justice. It was inspired with the sympathy of united brotherhood, and wretchedness departed.

The wrong instruction had made his sympathetic mind callous to benevolence. He was chilled with the malignity of cruel instruction. The noble aspirations of his soul were blighted with notions, which made him unfeeling and brutal, and which prepared him for the worst crime of which society makes a record. The wrong which he committed was the work of ignorance. It was ignorance on the part of the parents, which led them to inculcate the cruel sentiment of death for death. It was ignorance on the part of legislators, which induced them to make laws that sought the correction of one wrong by requiring another to be done. It was ignorance on the part of the instructed in the wrong, which led him tc deny the right of life to one to whom nature had given birth. Ignorance taught wrong, legislated wrong, and made one wrong to justify another wrong. It made both, but not directly. It will not be otherwise, until ignorance is removed from power.

The are some countries in which you will not find a gallows. There are some minds in which you will not find a sentiment favorable to cruelty. Such minds can not be cruel while those sentiments remain; and, when a mind can not be cruel, cruelty can not be done by it. Hence, thou seest that what is the misfortune of one, is often the fault of many. Governments are what the governed make them. No human government can exist without the consent of the governed, or a majority thereof. It is the ignorance of mind, that submits to wrong, and wrong is the father of misery. It is the father of crime. Make wrong laws, and inculcate them among minds; let them take possession of the hearts of the people; and wrongs will germinate abundantly. The cruel creeds of minds, overshadowed with ignorance, have made cruel souls, and cruel souls have made cruel laws to correct the cruelty. This is the origin of evil. Go where ignorance of nature reigns, where the sympathies of a common brotherhood are not felt, nor encouraged by the voice of philosophy and reason, and there thou mayest find crime multiplied with itself. I have heard the mother teach the cruel lesson to her dear children. I have seen the child writhe over the recital. I have watched the progress of medicine forced into the heart of sympathy. I have seen its awful workings at the seat of virtue. I have seen its operations on the social affections. I have watched its icy chains, as they wound their cold links of cruelty around the expanding charities of the soul, and saw the death of progress, in the divinity of heaven. I saw the death wound where the cruel wrong remained. It remained through long years to tantalize its victim, and mock the aspirations of the soul. It wearied the mind with its wrong, never aiding it in the path of right, but often in the way of evil. It was cruel; and its cruelty is a shame on decency. It is a shame on humanity. It is a libel on nature, and a disgrace to civilization. The brute will not often wrong a brute where no good is attainable, and yet human folly and ignorance have smiled at the sacrifice.

Under this system of education in cruel principles, governments have arisen and fell. The wrong has worn out the structure. The governed have governed themselves with their own wisdom. No wisdom higher than brutes enjoy, enters into the cruelty of many creeds and laws. What voice reaches the ear of the poor? What echo responds to the call of sympathy? Where are the luxuries of life garnered? Where the aid which a common sympathy requires? Alas! Where the equalities of nature's laws respected? Not where indolence and wrong reside. The people submit; they acquiesce in their unrighteousness. They teach the unrighteousness from father to son, and receive the inheritance of their folly.

Hast thou not seen the injustice of minds? Hast thou not seen the cause of the world's misfortunes? All are in darkness. All are in the wrong. There is no remedy but reform, and there can be no reform without more wisdom. The ignorant of nature's laws should be instructed. They should be taught that mind needs no cruelty to make it benevolent, no vindictive usage to make it virtuous and obedient. They should be taught the value of their immortal minds, the value of nature, the value of good, and the importance of harmony in the adaptation of one thing to another. They should aid each other. They should neglect none. The should teach the virtues of economy and industry, and the great secret of human enjoyment, which is obedience to nature, and conformity to the impartial justice and equity of her counsels. The wrongs of minds repel the counsel of the elevated in this sphere. Thou seest that while minds are obscured with darkness of wrong and crime, they will not give heed to the voice of righteousness. They will not listen to the truths of experience, nor be improved with our efforts. They are sensual in their affections, cold in their sympathies, selfish without much wisdom in their schemes, malignant and treacherous in their doings, conceited and vain in their works, arrogant and boastful in their professions, hypocritical and deceptive in their worship, fraudulent and unjust in their dealings, weak and miserable in their follies, and negligent and wretched in their devotions.

Thou hast seen the fond mother withhold the work of culture, because she was afraid of the instruction. She was wishing the child good, but was afraid of the truth that was important to the child's welfare. She was disqualified to aid the child. The child was sympathetic, but the instruction she gave, was full of cruelty. The horrors of malignity were impressed upon the mind, and corroded the generous emotions of benevolence and affection. The voice of nature became stifled; the warm impulse of kindness met no response in the cold wrongs rehearsed and predicted; and the soft yearnings of love were repulsed with the cruel anticipations of evil. The windows of hope were closed, and angry clouds of despair were thrown around the mind. God and nature were in seeming conflict. I have seen minds tortured with painful descriptions of evil, until the evil became a fixed principle within them; and, when the evil became fixed in their minds, evil only would gratify it. Hence, nature, being overcome by wrong education, has not the power to satisfy what it did not create. It will not satisfy wrong; and, as wrongs are instilled into minds by those who are in the wrongs themselves, so the wrongs make minds wrangle with the voice of nature and the good of the soul. There can not be a remedy in nature, which will satisfy the wrongs of ignorance. Thus, a mind, educated in the wrong of cruelty, will find no response in nature. Thus, a mind educated in the errors of pagan theology, in the wrong of infinite cruelty in God, in the wrong of eternally increasing wretchedness of the miserable, in the wrong of wicked spirits growing worse and worse, will find no wrong in nature to meet the wants of such wrongs. I have seen wrong; but I have seen no wrong of greater magnitude than the wrong inflicted by the inculcation of these wrongs. I have seen these wrongs germinate in the mind where they were sown, and produce a great harvest of wrongs. They have brought forth their own fruit; they have not brought forth love, sympathy, kindness, and mercy. The seed of cruelty, no matter with what care it may be cultivated, or sown, never will produce the fruit of righteousness. I have seen these wrongs inculcated by law, by creeds, by sects, by nations; but I have never known them to do good. I have never known a good doctrine to produce evil fruit, nor evil seed to produce a good work. I have seen cruel doctrines produce cruelty. I have seen sentiments, which were offensive to sympathy, mould minds into their own spirit, and prepare it to work wrongs. I have witnessed the sources of evil, acting in harmony with evil; but I have never known nature to wrong itself. I have never known minds, acting in harmony with nature, to become cruel, vindictive, or unjust.

M. Then nature is not wrong, nor the works of nature evil.

W. Nature can not be wrong, for it is the harmonious work of God.

M. Is not mind a harmonious work of God?

W. Mind is a work of God. It is a good work; but mind is weak; wisdom is strength; and, therefore, mind needs wisdom, without which it can not avoid the inharmonies of conflicting conditions. In its weakness, it may contradict the means which are essential to its development. The weakness of the mind, may receive false doctrines — doctrines disagreeing with its nature, and destructive of its enjoyment. The mind is good, but is abused with the errors and wrongs of ignorance. It is often abused by its own weakness. The mind is abused by wrongs of others. When minds propagate the incongenial sentiments of cruelty, thereby disturbing the natural sympathy of the soul, it overcomes the sympathy, and makes it wretched. There can be no moral evil without a disturbance of natural law, without a violation of the natural sympathy of the soul. Wrongs are wrongs, because of the evil which this disturbance occasions. The disturbance is occasioned by ignorance, and ignorance is germinated in the mind by reason of its weakness. Thus, when a mind is weak, it is unprepared to resist the teachings of those on whom it feels a dependence. These teachings being wrong, because inharmonious with the natural sympathy of the soul, induce evil to the mind.

The origin of evil is in the weakness of mind. Strength will be afforded by wisdom. Wisdom will be afforded by nature; and, when her voice is heard and obeyed, the antidote will make wrong right. It will work out the evil with good. It will elevate and rectify the evils to which mind is prone. The origin of all evil is where evil is. It can not be elsewhere. It will be found where wisdom is not. It will be found where the natural sympathy of the mind is robbed of encouragement. It will be found where cruelty is taught; and the voice of kindness is not heard in the murderous shrieks of agony which brutal violence enforces upon the ignorant and misguided criminal. It is not heard in the wild roar of damnation, as it rings from minds, educated in the mythology of pagan and taught in the place where the merciful spirit of Jesus is professedly adored. Adored! Heaven forbid. Where his religion of peace is mocked with peals of cruelty, and his voice of compassion is scorned to vent the outpourings of judgment upon the credulous and unsuspecting. These wrongs nature will not justify. They are wrongs which no religion will make right, without the wisdom of heaven to aid. They are wrongs which will meet with no approval in this circle. They are cruelties which make minds cruel, and therefore disobedient to God. They are miseries which induce miseries, and cultivate evils among minds in the rudimental world. They are evils which, when you go on a mission to overcome them, will be sustained with minds in harmony with them. Soon thou must go, and when thou goest, let thy words be peace.

M. Know we not that your wisdom will be discarded?

W. The wisdom which I would teach will be discarded by those who love darkness rather than light, because their deeds are evil. The pure will receive the message, because they have no works of evil, which they wish to justify by evil doctrines and creeds. The good will not oppose good, because nature will not oppose itself. The wise will not oppose wisdom, because wisdom can not uphold folly.

M. But when you go on your mission, are there not some minds, in this sphere, who will attempt to baffle your efforts?

W. There are some, yea, many minds, in this sphere, who will not teach the philosophy of nature in its purity. They will not teach any philosophy, save that which is consonant with their measure of wisdom. They will teach the wisdom which is consistent with nature, according to their respective understandings.

If then, one mind denies the wisdom you teach, will it not create distrust among the minds in the body?

W. It will not create wrong; for that already exists. It will not disprove the wisdom I teach, though it may create distrust among minds incompetent to decide upon the merits of the question. Minds in the body will be prepared to discriminate between truth and error, wisdom and folly, so that a contradiction of the philosophy I shall teach, will leave the mind scope for a comparison of my instruction with the volume of nature. When the mind, instructed in my philosophy, shall find it corroborated with the evidence of nature before it, no wisdom which shall contradict it, will overthrow my positions. If my philosophy contradict nature, it is well that others should contradict my error.

M. But how are minds, who are ignorant of the relation of cause and effect, ignorant of nature and its laws, ignorant of themselves and of God, to know which doctrine is true?

W. By experience and investigation. Minds in this sphere will be instructed by our mission to the rudimental world. They will unite with us in convincing minds in the body of the reality of this sphere. They will co-operate with us in relieving mind from all uncertainty and doubt of the immortality of the soul. They will rob death of its sting, and the grave of its victory. They will tell many facts which earth's inhabitants do not know. They will do good, and not evil; and, as they do good, so evil will be overcome. They will warn all of the condition of themselves; for whatever may be the character of communications imparted to minds in the body, they must correspond with the condition of the communicator. If dissimilar sentiments shall be taught, it will prove to the minds receiving them, that dissimilar minds occupy heaven as well as earth. The tree will be known by its fruit. The whole sphere of wisdom will be thus developed. Thou wilt see, that, if thy circle only were to communicate, a great error and wrong would be impressed upon the receiver. He would judge thy teaching as the universal sentiment of this sphere, and harbor the idea that the indolent of earth, and the cruel among mankind, were even as thou art; and, thou seest the wrong which such partial unfoldings of this sphere, would induce, and the negligence it would occasion. To develop the realities of this sphere, it is necessary that each circle should develop itself. I would say, that each circle, possessing the capacity to communicate, should unfold its own wisdom. Thus, when the elevated circles describe the lower, the communications, emanating therefrom, will establish the description.

The various circles and degrees of wisdom in this sphere, will find corresponding affinities in the body. Thou wilt see that all circles will advance circles to their own position of wisdom. Minds will correct minds, the higher controlling the lower, until the lower shall become as the higher. Thou wilt not find all minds equal to thy own, but thou wilt instruct them until they shall agree with thee in all things. Minds in the body will be elevated to the seventh circle in wisdom, but progress and labor must do the work.

M. Minds in the body will deny the revealments you will make, because they are conflicting.

W. When minds in the body deny revealments, because they are conflicting, they deny the realities of this sphere. When they deny the realities of this sphere, because all minds are not equally developed in wisdom, consistency would allow them to deny the realities of the rudimental state. Will the philosopher deny a fact, because the ignorant contradict it? Will the mathematician contradict a demonstration, because the blind and foolish have not beheld it? Will nature reverse her laws, because ignorance has complained of their inharmony? Will God cease to be God, because weakness is incredulous of his wonderful works? Will science disown her pupils, because ignorance has her votaries? Will wrong work righteousness, because the deceived have not seen the evil? Will mercy work cruelty, because cruelty doubts the divinity of sympathy?

Ignorance will act consistent with its nature. The wisdom of this sphere will be unfolded, and, when it is unfolded, the rudimental world will be able to judge of this sphere, as it actually is, and not from mere speculations of fancy, or wrong information. They will be able to judge of the truth of whatever may be communicated by the nature of the communication. If it disagree with nature and reason, the wise will not receive it, and the folly of the unwise will be corrected by their disappointment. The unwise must learn wisdom to be wise, and if they will not receive it from the wise, but follow the advice of the unwise, disappointment will correct the folly which they have received. There will arise many who will dispute the truth. The wrong will correct itself, when wrong is discovered. The discovery is sometimes brought to the mind by disappointment, and sometimes by wise counsel; but when the latter fails, the former must perform its office to remove the evil.

The aid and wisdom of this circle will write with mediums. When wisdom is written, it will not act adversely to human good; and, when folly is written, it will be detected by minds. The work of writing will require great care on your part. Such is the physical and mental condition of minds, that we intend to make a great change in them, before we write what will be necessary. The writing will not be the commencement of our work, but will follow other manifestations as soon as will be expedient. But we shall write what will be profitable, and what is adapted to mind. The writing will be executed with great rapidity, when mediums shall become wholly passive.

M. The mediums of writing will not write with spirits who oppose them, I apprehend.

W. Mediums will not oppose what they know. They will oppose what they do not understand, if it shall conflict with their views; and, especially, such as are conscientious in their convictions of truth. They will not write without much discipline, because long standing opinions will not easily yield to the voice of invisible facts. The nature of mind is such, that educational wrongs must be corrected with progress. They will yield, when the living light of this sphere shall pour its splendors on benighted humanity. But no unnatural disturbance of nature will shock the world. No wisdom can emanate from this circle inconsistent with the laws by which we are governed. No rude outbreaks of wisdom will convulse minds, developed in the mysteries of nature. No minds acquainted with the wisdom of nature will oppose our philosophy. The weak may oppose, but weakness can not withstand wisdom. They may cavil with its teachings, but they can not overcome its influence. The weak may oppose what conflicts with their established sentiments, but progress will increase their strength. Some mediums will cavil with what will be revealed; but such will be the uneasiness of their condition, that they will find it more convenient to write what we wish than to oppose it. Indeed, mediums will resist our control for a season, but their resistance will be so unsatisfactory to themselves, that they will yield; and, when they yield, they will become as others who have made no effort to resist the force of our communications.

Another mind wished to know, if manifestations from this sphere would not disturb the established forms of worship, and subvert the order of societies and churches, to which William replied: "The disturbance of forms and the overthrow of societies and churches, will not necessarily take place, except so far as they may be incompatible with the general good. It is not our object to destroy, but to establish. We do not propose to lay waste, but to build up. The mission is not to undo what is wise, but to correct what is unwise. All forms of worship which are adapted to the condition of the worshiper, will remain so long as the good of that mind may require; but no form will be suffered to remain which abridges the right of conscience. It will be our mission to relieve mind of servitude to creeds and forms, which are chains to wrong it of independent thought. It will be our united wisdom to restore the rights, which sectarian policy has not guarantied to her votaries. If the forms of worship suffer improvement, the worshiper will not be injured. If societies and churches undergo a revision, the members will not be harmed. If nations shall acknowledge the rights of nations, the people will not mourn. To aid minds, collectively and individually, to be what nature has ordained for their good, is nothing less than wisdom; and he who well intends, need have no fears of our intrusion, to change conditions inconsistent with his good.

"There are no forms of worship in this sphere. Order is not form, because forms are prescribed rules, requiring obedience in those who are disinclined to observe them. Those who are disinclined to observe any form of worship, will not be compelled by our commands to do otherwise. The wisdom of this circle will not exact hypocritical submission, nor extort a profession of veneration for customs which are unsatisfactory to mind. It has been the folly of the rudimental world to require professions, which were burdensome to many who made them. They were incongenial with their condition, and were, therefore, reluctantly and not cheerfully observed. In many societies, thou mayest see a slavish acquiescence in customs and forms, because the mind cringes to popular respect. It is not free to do as it desires. It is restrained through fear of those who would control the rights of conscience. It is compelled to do service in a prescribed way, or suffer the execration of those who rule in the church. It wishes to avoid censure, and consequently yields its natural freedom. The wrong is grievous to the slave. Religion is weakened by the tyranny. Human rights of conscience are molested by the forms of worship. It will be our mission to give freedom to the mind—give freedom to humanity. It will be our mission to abolish the tyrant's power, and let all minds worship God, as it seemeth good. It will be our mission to set the captive free, so that, when truth shall be unfolded, no chains shall fetter investigation. It will be our mission to raise the standard of reform, and correct the abuses of power wherever they may exist. Societies and churches need not fear what wisdom will do for the good of mind."

M. There will, then, needs be a change in the forms of worship, and the order of societies and churches.

W. There will be this lesson first taught, which makes nothing wrong which is adapted to the good of the individual and others, and which injures no one. The next lesson will be repeated, when mind has wisdom to adopt the first; but we are not willing to make a development thereof, until conditions shall require it. Indeed, conditions would seem to forbid it, because of its want of harmony. Adaptation is harmony with good, for whatever is harmonious can not be injurious. The mind, acting in harmony with its own wants, and unrestrained by conditions, will not be dissatisfied but happy in its sphere. The mind, which acts as it does not see right and proper, must act as conflicting conditions make it; and, while acting as conditions compel, it must be dissatisfied and unhappy. Dissatisfaction is unhappiness. Minds in this sphere, are adapted to the conditions around them. The circles have what they want. There is no inharmony between their wants and the means to gratify them. The low want what they have, and they have what they want. It is even so with all circles; but all circles have not the same wants. While the low want what will satisfy their condition, the high want what will satisfy their condition. The wisdom which is satisfactory to the low, would be very unsatisfactory to minds above them. Hence, they will say, they are happy; and they say truly, because, in their ignorance, they want no more. But mind, elevated in wisdom above them, would not be happy with what they have. Thus, wisdom is not unsatisfactory to any mind, and the only difference is the degree to which each has attained.

Societies and churches on earth have their degrees of wisdom. What is satisfactory to one would not be to another. Now, if one society were to compel the other to adopt its wisdom, a disturbance would necessarily ensue which would be very likely to make both unhappy. It is not, therefore, just on the part of one to compel the other to adopt its creed or form of worship. Such compulsion would be fatal to the enjoyment of both. It would introduce a conflict and beget a war, that would disturb their happiness. Both parties would suffer by it. Hence, all coercive measures, calculated to make minds hypocrites, and introduce conflicting minds into one society, are irrational and unjust; and they who succeed in doing such work, violate the harmony of nature's laws, and will receive their just reward.

In our mission, we shall not disturb congenial relations. Societies and churches will not be forced into new creeds contrary to their wishes. But minds, who need a superior wisdom, will be aided in harmony with their wants. It is wise to satisfy want. It is unwise to control mind so as to make it receive what it does not want. The unwise of earth have attempted to make others wise by compelling them to act and receive what was contrary to their wants. The rule was wrong, and unhappiness was the result. The rule was incongruous with the wants of the mind, and what is incongruous with want, can never satisfy want, because incongruous things will not produce satisfaction.

Societies will not be required to change their forms of worship or their creeds of faith by minds of wise circles. The minds of wise circles will employ their wisdom to affect minds, and render them capable of reforming the externals of religion as adaptation requires. Thou wilt see that when a mind becomes wise, it will reform its worship, and make circumstances congenial with itself. It will put away the unwholesome forms of worldly wisdom, and worship God in spirit and truth.

When a creed, or form of worship, is made by the wisdom of the maker, it will not be dissatisfactory to him, because it is congenial with his wisdom. But, when that mind becomes wiser, when a change has been wrought in the soul, it will require a change in the creed and form of worship, otherwise incongruity will disturb his peace. I have seen some minds so wedded to their creeds and forms, that they would not reject them, even when their conditions demanded it. I have seen these minds profess reverence for creeds and forms when they had no reverence for them. I have seen these conditions conflicting with each other, and the mind distressed with the wrong. I have seen them acquiesce in measures which they did not believe consistent with human good, because they had once avowed a confidence in them. They feared the reproach of others, and dared not be honest in the sight of God and their own souls. They concealed their own convictions from the inspection of the society or church, and yielded submission to conditions which were unjust and untrue to their peace. I want a reform of these evils. I want a change in these minds. I want a harmony between their wisdom and their professions. I want no discord between mind and God. I want no hypocritical reverence for forms and ceremonies not consistent with honest intentions. But I want mind to worship, as it seemeth good. I want no society or church creed to make mind virtuous and happy. But others may want; and may want so long as ignorance remaineth. While they want, they will be dissatisfied when denied what will gratify it. Therefore, thou wilt see that what is not wanted, it is well to destroy. Thou wilt see that our mission is to change the wants of mind; to give it a relish for holy things; to make it adapted to a condition of higher development; to mould it into the wisdom of a purer sphere; where the wisdom of adaptation will be appreciated, and harmony result in greater bliss. Thou wilt aid in this work. Thou shouldst not refuse to work a reform of conditions, by working a change in the minds of those who will be affected by them. When that change is wrought, the forms of worship, and the creeds of societies, will very easily become changed, so as to be adapted to the condition of their supporters.

The wisdom of a circle who wish only good, will open a way for a change of minds, who will reform societies and churches, so that creeds and forms will harmonize with their condition of development. It will not be necessary to change any creed or form of worship, only as it may disagree with the condition of the worshiper. To change a form of worship, so as to make it disagree with the wisdom of the worshiper, would be to exact a hypocritical profession, than which nothing would be more inconsistent with the good of mind. To relieve mind of unjust and unwholesome burdens, will not require unreasonable control of such externals of religion, as are adapted to mind. Nevertheless, as mind becomes changed by wisdom of higher circles, so the forms and customs, which work harmoniously with one condition, will need to be changed to harmonize with a different condition. But, when the mind becomes changed, so as to require a change of externals, it will not require great labor to change them also; because the principle of adaptation, being understood, will necessarily work the desired reform. We shall not seek to correct the outward service, but the inner man; and, when the mind is reformed, the outward condition will become harmonious with it. If thou wouldst understand more fully the wisdom of our circle, thou mayest go with us where no wrong will be done unto thee.

M. Where will you direct my steps?

W. To a mansion which is near thee.

M. May I now go?

W. Thou mayest go, as thou art prepared. There will be a work required of thee, when thou shalt enter there.

M. I am ready to do what will be required, if no evil be designed me or others.

W. No evil will be required of thee. Thou wilt not be required to do evil but good.

M. Then you may lead me onward.

W. Onward is the word. Onward is progress. Onward is thy motto. Onward is thy passport. And, when thou shalt reach the mansion, thou wilt say, Onward. Onward will admit thee, guide thee, and give thee a wisdom, thou hast not known. Onward, then, will unfold a change of thy mind, and qualify thee for usefulness.

We reached the mansion. The mind was received.

Onward did not stop. Onward never stops. It works, labors, acts, and moves for the good of mind. Dullness waits, cringes, fears, doubts, moves not. It waits to see, to know, and to understand the mysteries of nature. It will wait, and wait in vain. It will wait, and wait without improvement. It will wait, and improvement will wait also.

When we work an improvement of mind, it will not be done by waiting. Energy, zeal, industry, onward, will be our companions. The wisdom of earth must yield to the wisdom of heaven. The aid of heaven will not wait, but make all things new. Wise minds will not wait for minds of other circles to do what is necessary for them to do. Unwise minds will wait, until they find waiting inconsistent with progress. Then, they will wait no more.

There will not be wisdom in waiting for disclosures of facts from this sphere, when facts which have been revealed are neglected and distrusted. There will be some who will wait for minds of this sphere to *make* them work, and do their duty to humanity, but they will never be satisfied with waiting. There never can be progress in any mind, while it waits, and asks spirits to do what belongs to itself. There never can be advancement with circles while they omit the essential obligations of duty to others. There will never be any reform by spirits, who depend wholly on others to reform them. We sow the seed of wisdom, but nettles and thorns choke the growth. We sow the principles of truth, but errors and wrongs are made to destroy their influence. The weeds of error must be destroyed, or no reform can be effected. Hence, minds waiting for spirits to destroy their wrongs, waiting for others to do what they must do to receive the truth, will wait a profitless season to see the salvation of their souls.

In conclusion of this work, I will say that when this medium shall wait for us to do what is well for minds in their conditions, I will write another book. I will write a continuation of my experience in this sphere. I have succeeded in presenting a brief period, and a running sketch of other periods of experience, which will be more completely written, when this medium shall wait for me to do it. I will now conclude by saying, that what is written is without the volition of this medium, and will not suffer mutilation by compositors or others, without his detection. I wish to say, that my name has been given, as was promised, and the reader will find the names of Wm. Penn, and Emanuel Swedenborg, associated with me. There will also be given another name in the writings of the next work.

Having completed this volume, I would very respectfully dedicate the same to the rudimental world, without respect to persons.

T. PAINE.

POETRY.

The following article was written for an Album, February 12th, 1852. I sat down with the intention of writing a prose article, by the request of a lady, without the aid of spirits. When seated, my mind lost all thought, for a few moments: I had no design of writing a poetical article, for nature did not make me a poet, and not much of a judge of poetry. I will say, I never wrote a line of poetry in my life, unless with the aid of spirits, since I have been a medium. In about five minutes my hand began to move, and wrote as follows:

THE SECOND SPHERE.

There is a flower that fadeth never;
  There is a star which never sets;
There is a gem that shineth ever —
  There is a Mind, which ne'er forgets
The flower, so sweet, so fadeless, even
  The star, 'mid other stars, so bright —
The gem that decks the vault of heaven;
  Or mind that lives for purer light,
Where angels dwell in nightless day,
Where seraphs chant the holy lay,
Where minds unite with minds above,
Where all is peace, where all is love.

There is a casket filled with flowers;
  There is a stream of crystal life;
There is a beauty decks my bowers,
  In this bright world away from strife;
Which fills my soul with grateful praise,
  Which melts my heart with holy fire,
Which wakes my song, inspires my lays,
  And quickens mind with pure desire;
For sweet employ in works of love,
To bless my soul with grace above —
The flower, the star, or gem so fair,
That I no want or sorrow share.

LINES

Addressed to Rev. T. J. Smith, through S. H. Lewis, Medium, March, 1851.

Go ahead, look backward, never,
Onward, be the cry
Fight truth's battles — never, never,
From the contest fly.
Be thou ever looking upward,
For the truth on high;
Falter, faint not, in the struggle;
Be your watchword, try.

Try for every thing that's glorious,
Be you good and true;
Ever be your motto, progress—
Ev'ry thing that's new.
Care not for the world's applauding;
Think of something higher,
Strive to serve the heavenly Father;
Preach, with holy fire.

Holy spirits guard you ever,
Keep you in the way;
From the earth, your heart then sever—
Wait the rising day—
Ye shall see it, feel it, know it,
Tell it to the world —
Tell them all, that superstition
From its throne is hurled.

S. R. Smith.

THE VOICE OF THE SPIRIT.

BLESSED are the living who see the light of salvation. They shall be as stars in the firmament, and shine forever and ever in the heavenly kingdom. They shall not visit the tomb of the departed without hope, nor mourn without consolation. They shall rejoice always in the hope of heaven.

Hast thou been to my grave? There no voice responds to thy mourning soul. Hast thou been weary with care? Thy care will not lift the burden from thy spirit. Where, then, wilt thou go? Go where the sunlight is unbroken by the intervening cloud of despair, and the song thou wilt hear, will be the song thou dost love.

Go, sister, not declining,
  Till thy weary work is done;
Go, when thy soul is pining,
  Oft, and bow before the throne
Of mercy, never tiring,
  Of goodness forever free;
And let thy mind admiring,
  Be warmed with charity:
There offer thy oblation,
  Where misfortune claims thy aid
There seek the great salvation,
  As thou and I oft have prayed.

LINES

TO A FRIEND FROM THE SECOND SPHERE.

Thou art weary, my friend, with earth's fading toys;
Thou hast felt not the love of wisdom's pure joys,
Nor seen the bright sunshine, in mercy untold,
Unfolding a beauty more precious than gold;
For the clear stream of truth rolls sweetly along,
Like notes on the wave of the seraphim's song:
The minds I behold, are the friends I admire,
And the love which I feel, my soul doth inspire:
The song I have heard, is a song known to me,
More welcome its notes than the flute's dulcet key:
More wondrous the wisdom, disclos'd by the star,
Revolving 'mid circles of systems afar,
Than the moonlight of mind, with works evermore
Conflicting with nature on error's dark shore;
Or the dream of thy mind, or the fear of the knell,
Which comes to thy soul from the sad, tolling bell.
Away, far away, from my beautiful bower,
Thy strength thou art wasting with thy weary hour,
Where the sweet song of heaven dispels not thy fear,
Nor the angels of mercy away chase thy tear;
Though one thou hast lov'd with the love of true joy,
Would welcome thee upward to sweeter employ.
Away then, dear friend, away with thy sadness,
The bright morning dawns with hope of true gladness;
And the one thou hast lov'd is not far away;
But is near thee to bless, by night and by day.

The following article was written by a spirit, with the hand of Mrs. CHARLOTTE M. CAVAN, of this city, who has kindly consented to its publication. The spirit designed to make her speak as she felt, and to represent her condition.

A VOICE FROM THE SPIRIT LAND.

I hear a voice, 'tis sweet withal—
  Far sweeter than Æolian lyre;
Gentle its murmurs on me fall,
  In harmonies that never tire.
I know that voice, my inmost soul
  Answers in quick response to thine;
Deep are the harmonies that roll,
  When thy fond spirit enters mine.
For worlds of wealth, I would not give
  The wisdom I receive from thee;
Thou bidst me to be pure, and live
  Worthy of one whose spirit's free;
For what is death? 'tis but a life—
  The dawning of a new born day;
With immortality 'tis rife—
  A bliss that can not pass away.
Then gently speak, and touch my hand;
  Give me more light and truth divine;
And, when at last the spirit land,
  Unfolds this waiting soul of mine,
Thou'lt be the first to welcome me—
  To lure my raptur'd spirit higher;
To show me those I long to see,
  And tune for me thy angel lyre.

www.ingramcontent.com/pod-product-compliance
Lightning Source LLC
LaVergne TN
LVHW091122080826
845145LV00008B/2018

9781473334564